Three Key Success Factors for Transforming Your Business

Three Key Success Factors for Transforming Your Business

Mindset, Infrastructure, Capability

Michael Hagemann

BEP BUSINESS EXPERT PRESS

Three Key Success Factors for Transforming Your Business:
Mindset, Infrastructure, Capability

First published in 2020 by
Business Expert Press, LLC
222 East 46th Street, New York, NY 10017
www.businessexpertpress.com

ISBN-13: 978-1-95152-732-7 (paperback)
ISBN-13: 978-1-95152-733-4 (e-book)

Business Expert Press Human Resource Management and Organizational Behavior Collection

Collection ISSN: 1946-5637 (print)
Collection ISSN: 1946-5645 (electronic)

Cover image licensed by Ingram Image, StockPhotoSecrets.com

Cover and interior design by Exeter Premedia Services Private Ltd., Chennai, India

First edition: 2020

10 9 8 7 6 5 4 3 2 1

Printed in the United States of America.

Abstract

There are now many different Change Management models. Some are very complex; some are not very effective.

With the MIC model (MIC = Mindset, Infrastructure, Capability) there is an easy-to-understand and easy-to-use model presented that has proven itself many times over in practice. It is useful in both private and business settings, in both large transformation projects as well as smaller change projects.

In order to keep MIC application-oriented, in the second part of this book a change and project management approach called PACE has been introduced that describes a step-by-step approach of how MIC can be implemented more linearly in project-driven changes.

Every change requires the right mindset, the right infrastructure, and the necessary capabilities.

MIC comes from practice and is for practice.

The book is aimed at consultants and managers, HR managers and project managers who need to lead or implement change programs. Executives and their teams will benefit from the book as much as individuals who want to change or face change in their lives. Finally, it addresses all those who watch the changes of our time and are curious to understand more deeply how changes do not have to be passively endured but can be actively understood and lived as an opportunity.

Everybody will face change at some point. MIC will help see change no longer as something threatening, but a way to accept change and integrate into life.

Keywords

change; change management; leadership; transformation; emotional intelligence; mindset; leading change; managing change; restructuring; culture

Contents

Foreword I

This book for leaders and practitioners is exceptional. It seamlessly integrates a very practical action-orientation on how to implement change in organizations, together with thoughtful reflections on considerable experience, as well as demonstrating a deep understanding of science and theory, both past and present.

Hagemann's book is one of the few contributions among thousands of books on change management that is not only multidimensional but also personally authentic. It focuses on helping people and leaders in companies, large and small, deal with the dramatic and ever accelerating change affecting them and their societies. The author provides a toolkit, case studies and uses direct quotes from those both undergoing and implementing change to supplement his foundational framework and road map. He shows why and how leaders need to keep in mind, and work on, three critical areas in order to make change sustainable and successful.

Hagemann introduces a new framework for change management that he refers to as the MIC model. He shows how every change requires the right mindset (M), the right infrastructure (I), and the necessary capabilities (C) to make change successful. Mindset is more than just an attitude—it's broader, "incorporating, purpose, spirit, soul, and intellect." Infrastructure (I) refers to all physical and mental elements which encourage, support, and enhance a behavior. Physical infrastructure includes the office environment, IT, processes, assessments, development, and organizational infrastructure. By capability (C), he refers to ability, competence, and suitability. The book provides leaders with a step-by-step and very thorough description of the processes and tools on how to implement the MIC change model.

Michael Hagemann is an authentic leader and a reflective practitioner. Today he is Vice President in charge of Change Management at Deutsche Post DHL Group, one of the leading global logistics providers, a company with about 550,000 employees and total assets of 50 billion euros. For many years he was a priest and an academic director for international adult education in the Catholic Church. After taking a sabbatical he writes that he "completed a radical, personal re-orientation and evolved himself into a change and transformation manager for corporate consulting, educational organizations as well as with NGO's." He does not shy away from using his own experience of personal change in portraying the emotional toll change can have on people as well as organizations and companies.

Hagemann went on to gain an MBA, complimented by numerous certifications in Six Sigma, DISC, Mindfulness, and Neuro Linguistic Programming (NLP). His direct experience in the world of business is rooted in his 10 years in his present role at DPDHL, one of the largest privately held companies in the world. Its remarkable growth journey includes many initiatives with serious and large-scale change efforts. From the early 1990s, this company underwent, and continues to undergo, major transformations, from a 500-year-old government-owned postal service (Deutsche Post) to a company that is 80 percent owned by international private investors. And without doubt, DPDHL is one of the most global of companies today—with a presence in almost all countries and territories.

On a more personal level, I have been witness to several of the company's transformational changes, evolution, and its approach to change and growth. From a modest start in 1990, by the mid-1990s the company began to initiate significant leadership development and executive education to assist its integration process. Leaders were trying to learn faster than the rate of change, analyzing how best to tackle the myriad of issues that accompany rapid expansion and integration. At one point they were acquiring as many as five or so companies every month. And so they looked to the outside to examine as many good change management practices worldwide as they could, including those at GE and others at the time, to understand what might help them manage this dramatic transition. I raise this point to provide context, that Hagemann's book is based on a thorough understanding of other major company experiences together with the experience of his own company's dramatic change and transformation.

What also makes this book different from others is the consistent reference to ensuring that morality, ethics, and human values are an essential part of the change management process. With wisdom and compassion the author counsels leaders that manipulation is unacceptable and counterproductive—ethical behavior must always be at the center of decision-making and change management. This approach is inspiring, very relevant, and now much more acceptable in our post "shareholder value" era. Hagemann's perspective, like the rest of the book, puts his contribution on change management far ahead of other approaches—it is an outstanding and very relevant model for those wanting to implement change management for the 21st century.

Dr. Yury Boshyk
CEO
Global Executive Learning
Chairman, The annual Global Forum on
Strategic Change, Leadership and Learning

Foreword II

It is no longer a secret that change management has become a success factor for all types of change processes. More so, change management has become such a hype that the market seems to be literally flooded with lots of new books on theoretical methods and models or practical tips and guidelines. There is hardly any book that has developed into a standard work so far that one "must have read"; may be due to the fact that it is extremely difficult, on the one hand, to develop universal theories preferably which, on the other hand, can be applied to an almost limitless number of different situations and contexts.

The present change management has evolved from the classical organization development. As organization development is a discipline, which has been around for nearly as long as organizations are analyzed, structured, and developed—namely since over 60 years—one cannot say that change management is a new discipline. The reasons why change management has experienced a renaissance in recent years lie in the major, extensive, and extremely rapid changes, which are increasingly impacting our present. With the use of new technologies like powerful computers, broadband networks, and smartphones, which can be taken everywhere, it is not just work environments that have changed drastically but also see this change in our private lives.

This book presents a new change model, which focuses on the three most important areas of every change—mindset, infrastructure, capability (MIC). In the process, the author does not just manage to integrate and diversify existing theories and models. The MIC model also includes long-standing and extensive experience with practical application of the most varied models and theories. Thus, it is not surprising that the model presented is comprehensible at the first go and seems plausible.

The major problem with present change management models and methods is that they are either too generally valid to be applied in special situations and to be able to derive concrete recommendations for action, or that they are so special that they are only valid for specific

situations and therefore cannot be applied to a broad field of application. The methods mentioned first are usually—not least because of
their major possibility of application—well-founded theoretically and
empirical, which especially increases their scientific value; however, it
does not lead to their better practical application. Whereas, methods that
have been developed for special situations frequently lack theoretical–
empirical basis. They are usually more akin to case studies and cannot be
applied or can only be applied with difficulty to other situations due to their
uniqueness. The MIC model is an excellent combination of a higher-level
structure, which leads to wider applicability, and a tailor-made specificity,
from which clear recommendations for action can be derived for individual change situations. Therefore, the three main areas of mindset, infrastructure, and capability are not just explained at a higher level. Every
area is broken down into individual aspects, substantiated with theories,
reinforced with case studies, and broken down into concrete, practically
applicable toolboxes. For this reason, the MIC model has the potential to
become a "Standard," which becomes a practical and useful companion of
change processes.

For the author of this book, Michael Hagemann, I wish that the
MIC model gains wide recognition and also practical application and
circulation.

Prof. Dr. Martin R. Wolf

Preface

There are now many different change management models. Some are very complex; some are not very effective.

With the MIC (mindset, infrastructure, capability) model, I present an easy-to-understand and easy-to-use model that has proven itself many times over in practice. It is useful in both private and business settings, in both large transformation projects as well as smaller change projects.

In order to keep MIC application-oriented (Figure 0.1), I will introduce in the second part of this book a change and project management approach called PACE that describes a step-by-step approach of how MIC can be implemented more linearly in project-driven changes.

Every change requires the right mindset, the right infrastructure, and the necessary capabilities. Mindset is not just an attitude. "Mind," with its broad meaning of spirit, soul, intellect, and purpose, leads to a greater meaning of mindset than the way of thinking, attitude, or mentality. Capability includes "capable," which means able, competent, or suitable. Capability incorporates ability, skill, aptitude, talent, or even resources depending on the context. Infrastructure also has different meanings, which have yet to evolve

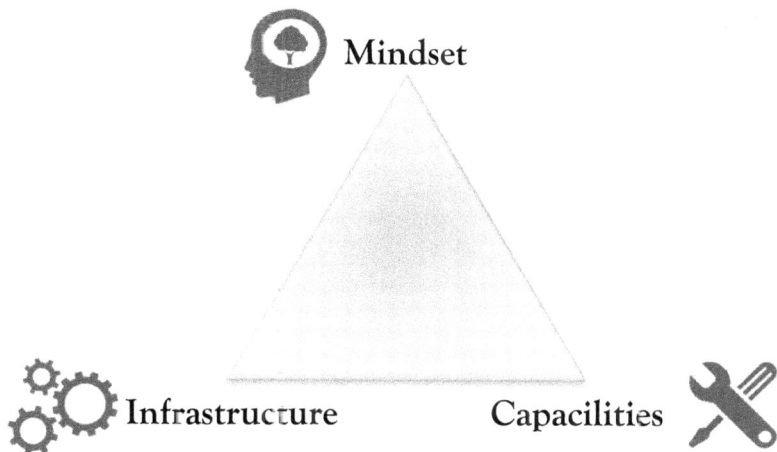

Mindset

Infrastructure   **Capacilities**

Figure 0.1 The MIC model

MIC comes from practice and is for practice. A colleague and I came up with the idea of formalizing the change approach, which we used more or less unconsciously for years. I am grateful to Robin Goel for many valuable conversations, from which MIC finally emerged as a model. I would also like to thank my colleague Sascha Cechlovsky for many opportunities for exchange of ideas, which have inspired and enriched me in the specification of the model and its writing. I would also like to thank all the other colleagues who have shown through the multiple uses of the model that it works—that change programs succeed if you follow and apply the MIC structure. Finally, I thank Dr. Hermann Wissing for intensive proofreading and fruitful exchange. Most of all, I thank my wife for always encouraging me to write down my thoughts, always having my back and keeping many evenings, nights, and weekends free for my writing.

The book is aimed at consultants and managers, HR managers, and project managers who need to lead or implement change programs. Executives and their teams will benefit from the book as much as individuals who want to change or face change in their lives. Finally, it addresses all those who watch the changes of our time and are curious to understand more deeply how changes do not have to be passively endured but can be actively understood and lived as an opportunity.

Everybody will face change at some point. MIC will help see change no longer as something threatening, but a way to accept change and integrate into life.

Michael Hagemann
December 8, 2019

CHAPTER 1

Introduction

There are many models, methods, and ideas around change management (CM). More and more new models are created and implemented. The CM consulting industry is growing continuously.

And yet CM remains an unsolved topic. No model was able to prevail; relevant books flood the market.

CM is and remains a virulent topic because it is ultimately about people; that those affected by the change are not overlooked, that someone takes care of them and shows them a way to handle the change and when change is increasing exponentially in all areas of life.

In both private and business, it seems difficult to find models or principles for the challenges of change that are readily applicable. The question of change design remains: What is the best way to manage change? As a rule, you start with the leaders. While there are rarely executives who negate the need for change, they still exist. Only recently did I hear a senior executive responding somewhat blankly to the question of whether CM access already exists: "We do not need Change Management. We *tell* people what to do and implement it." However, this kind of leadership is becoming less and less accepted. What impressed me a great deal a few years ago when I was allowed to get some insight into the management and leadership structure of the French army was the "mindset" of the officers, who expressly displayed a participatory and empowering style of leadership. All those who want to provide leadership in the 21st century need sooner or later to ask themselves how people can best be guided in and through change. Especially when the pressure to succeed is high and financial success must be achieved, the tendency for top-down instruction is great as it is still considered an excellent way to move an organization quickly toward success. Companies with more than 30 years of history work with silo structures and steep hierarchies. Most managers would prefer the achievement of financial goals to the rollout of soft, engaging change interventions, especially as they are usually measured exactly on the former.

The need to convince managers however to integrate CM into projects is becoming less common, and it has changed in the last 10 years, in our view. Today, I rather hear statements like these: "You do not need to convince me of CM, I know it's important; CM is so important that it has to be part of our daily tasks." So do projects need their own CM workstream? In practice, however, there are some arguments in favor of not forcing CM into a special workstream, but rather weaving it into various project activities. On the other hand, it often shows that CM is not self-propelling and—once initiated—does not evolve of its own accord. Instead, CM tends to disappear gradually unless explicitly promoted.

Maybe CM can be compared with communication. It is clear to everyone that in any case good communication should be provided and communication cannot be separated from other business life. Yet, if communication is not explicitly promoted in a department with appropriate leadership, it will not get the importance it deserves, and communication deficits will be the result.

Back to our question: How can change in companies best be managed? Some of the newer models, such as VUCA,[1] describe on a meta-level how to handle changes in our time. These models help to explain reality and prevent you from quickly engaging in inappropriate or unhelpful activities that do not help with the change. On the other hand, these models often do not provide tools, so their applicability is unclear. Other models are not concrete enough: Little stakeholder analysis, communication, and reflection on systemic change do not result in a valid behavioral change. A model is needed that *automatically* becomes part of every change and is easy to apply. We have used and implemented the MIC (Mindset, Infrastructure, Capability) model developed by myself in a wide variety of change formats, from smaller to complex cultural changes.

It can be used both as a structural model that describes basic principles for each change and as a toolbox from which the appropriate tools can be taken for any given change. The systemic change approach rightly

---

[1] Volatility, Uncertainty, Complexity, Ambiguity.

emphasizes that changes must always be seen in the overall context and that successfully implemented change takes the system as such into account. On the other hand, CM can also get lost in systemic analyses and processes which produce impressive system representations but little change.

When we talk about change, there are two dimensions; the differentiation is somewhat striking, but it is precisely in the rough-cut point of view that it becomes clear what this is all about.

On the one hand, there are the harsher elements of change: everything that has to do with new processes, new IT, new structures, new systems. On the other hand, it is about the human being, about behavior and mindset change, about an increased acceptance for change. Both factors do not behave additively but multiplicatively. They influence each other. $H \times S = R$ (hard times soft factors produce the result) is the simple change formula.

Toolbox

$$H \times S = R$$

The formula states: Hard times soft factors produce the result.

In every change, both factors are essential: A poorly structured and planned change does not contribute to success—even if one had generated a high level of acceptance. On the other hand, even the most well-planned change is doomed to failure without human acceptance.

A poorly planned change does not improve even with an increase in acceptance through CM and vice versa: The best project plan, the best new technology, the best new team structures will not be sustainable without a well-implemented change in behavior. For both cases, we see ample examples.

Case Study

A complex IT implementation did not fail because it was not sufficiently communicated or because not enough acceptance was generated.

On the contrary: Since the IT was over 40 years old and the process was largely analogous, due to filling in forms, there was a longing for the

> *new system. No change resistance was present. Instead a great openness and almost childlike waiting for Santa on Christmas morning. The IT application as such however did not work. Although users were extensively trained, it turned out that the software was too complicated and not sufficiently adapted to the needs of the company. CM could have been manipulative or improved feedback loops but that would not have been successful, according to the formula H × S = R, because the "hard" part of the change showed significant weaknesses.*

The other variation where a change is perfectly planned, but the soft factors are not taken into account, is probably more common. Of course, there are, as already mentioned, only a few managers who march in the old manner adopting to the motto: first comes the change, those affected will bow to it—or they can go. According to our observation however, there is also a pro forma integrated change approach. This is particularly evident in the fact that, first, the change budget is canceled whenever pressure increases or the change does not go as predicted. This reveals where the real priorities lie. A bit of communication, a bit of *Why* and *What*, that's enough. Practice shows that the change effectiveness here does not meet expectations because only pro forma change activities are carried out here, without thinking about actual change impact.

Leave the corporate context for a moment and enter the private sphere to face the challenge of personal behavioral change. Above all, we want to focus on changes that we have not chosen ourselves. The dictum attributed to Peter Senge, "People don't resist change, they resist being changed," makes it clear where the problem lies at the core of the change. Being a passive object and not a subject of change is not easy per se.[2]

Of course, there can also be internal resistance when I decide to change myself: a new job, a move, a new partner, a new resort. When these changes are intrinsically motivated, they usually contain more positive energy that outshines uncertainties, ambiguities, and doubts. But it becomes clear what core change is all about: Overcoming resistances that arise when habitual behavior or thinking has to be changed. A new job

---

[2] The Latin origin of passive means "suffer."

implies new people, new structures, a new environment. The new creates uncertainty, since habitual behavior may no longer fit. A move suggests leaving a space, which gives security. As a rule, a new partner does not fall from the sky but trained behavioral and communication structures may no longer fit. Even a new holiday resort spreads, at least in the beginning, insecurity. Very nice to watch when new guests arrive: Questioning looks: is it okay here? Was the money properly invested? and so on.

The holiday example can show yet another dimension of change: the emotional balance. Whenever a change takes place, we must emotionally follow the change and at the same time strive for inner balance again. Innumerable investigations into the processing of strokes of fate but also unexpected happiness show that there are emotional rashes but after about 3 months the emotional level of feeling is back to where it was at the beginning. On the one hand, this is an excellent achievement of our limbic system, and on the other hand, one might regret that the happiness feeling is not lasting. The lottery millionaire and the suddenly disabled are emotionally after 3 months on almost the same level as before.

On holiday you can often observe the following: In general, tourists come back happy and elated from vacation, perhaps with some sadness that the beautiful time is over. Rarely do you hear vacationers say: That was a total waste of time and money, we should not have done that. Even after 14 days of rain in the mountains, with children stuck inside, only the occasional opportunity to go out for an hour and lots of time spent in the swimming pool, which would have been cheaper at home. Honest reactions are: "What a bummer, the most important time of the year did not go as desired. Next year we will go back to Mallorca ...." Desperately the good is sought: "We went out to eat a few times, it was enough for a trip" and so on. On the output side are money and the expectation of recovery and beautiful moments with the family on the Alm. On the revenue side something must be generated ("Thank God there was a nice swimming pool"), otherwise, there would be an emotional imbalance.

Emotionally regaining balance is a major challenge in change. Being aware of this is one of the tasks of CM.

Bringing about a change in behavior in a sustainable way is a challenge, which is necessary to change habit.

The fact that it usually does not work out as planned fuels the growth of a billion dollar industry. Take the example of the diet. Basically, it's easy: Do not eat more than your body needs, eat healthily, and do sport! Still, over 90 percent of all diets result in the yo–yo effect. It is about a profound behavioral change that only becomes sustainable when you use several levers at the same time: Everything has to be done to define a new mindset, then you need to train the ability to eat differently and to enjoy sport. Finally, the new behavior must be woven into everyday structures; transparency must be generated; and success must be measured. You can easily recognize the change model of this book here.

Even if you recognize the patterns and work simultaneously in all areas, creating a new habit remains a challenge. In particular, the time factor is important: The longer one has practiced a particular behavior, the more pronounced the neural connections that oppose the change become. The popular saying that a heavy smoker, even as a nonsmoker, will always remain a smoker reflects that once established neural highways cannot be overwritten quickly and sustainably with other neuron roads. In the corporate context, it is exactly the same: The sum of deep habits, assumptions, and beliefs are usually called culture. Cultural changes are some of the biggest change projects. The deeper the required behavioral change, the more the people required and the more complex the new behavior, the greater the chance that the change will not be sustained.

Complex projects of cultural change can succeed if they undertake concrete behavioral changes and, in the long term, adapt their attitudes, abilities, and necessary supportive infrastructure.

A truly sustainable induced change is convincing—in the private as well as in the enterprise context.

Let us state at this point:

- CM is more necessary than ever and has to be woven into the respective change.
- The CM formula is: $H \times S = R$.
- Even in self-chosen changes, change is a challenge.
- The biggest change challenges are those we did not choose.
- People always seek emotional balance to overcome cognitive dissonance.

- Successful CM establishes new behaviors that lead to new habits that influence a new culture.

Before we turn to the MIC model, we briefly look at the evolution of CM to outline the challenge of change today.

CHAPTER 2

Change Management in the 21st Century

History

Since human beings are at the center of CM, the development of CM is shaped by the findings of psychology and its reception in an economic context. Psychology itself has only been recognized as a science since the 19th century. In particular, behaviorism, constructivism, human and cognitive psychology have influenced psychology in the economy.

Two representatives are mentioned here prominently, as their influence is still evident today:

- **Kurt Lewin** (1898–1947) became known through the three "States of Change" and the "force field analysis." The three change states are: unfreezing, moving, and refreezing. They describe a process where Lewin has undergone all change measures: in the first part, existing organizations, processes, and measures are lifted; in the second, they are transferred to the new state; and in the third, it is ensured that the new measures are constitutive and continue to become part of the organization.
- **William Bridges** (1933–2013) describes the change levels as "ending, neutral zone, new beginning" and thus emphasizes a special aspect: CM is not just about changing something, but the "transition" is the crucial phase.

The 90s mark a change: From organizational development, the topic of CM becomes more and more prominent and thus finally a discipline of its own. The outstanding key drivers responsible for this development are Jeanenne LaMarsh, John Kotter, and Spencer Johnson.

- **Jeanenne LaMarsh** (*1943) developed new ideas in "Changing the Way We Change," especially on the topic of developing change competencies, resistance management, and CM concepts.
- **John Kotter** (*1947) still considered the change pope, even if his model has been criticized many times. His eight steps of change in "Leading Change" describe levels of change which are still considered relevant today.
- **Spencer Johnson** (1938–2017) was best known for "Who moved my Cheese?", a parable dedicated to the topic of how best to handle change.

In the earlier years of the 21st century, the number of articles and books on the subject of CM has increased incrementally, so that no one overview should be given here. The steady increase in publications on the subject shows how important it still is.

The Change Curve

In the 1960s, Swiss psychologist Elisabeth Kübler-Ross described the process that patients underwent in difficult, life-threatening situations or in any kind of loss experience, using different phases of the change curve. After the first shock, patients entered the "denial" phase; the disease was denied or displaced. After realizing that the illness or loss (e.g., of life!) was reality, they entered the aggression phase. At the lowest point, life despair is greatest. Then she observed that the patients began to reconcile and accept the situation so that the disease or loss could even be integrated into life (cf. Kübler-Ross 2003) (Figure 2.1).

This experience has been widely reviewed, confirmed, and accepted in the economy as an intrapsychic process that takes place in every change, so that it cannot be avoided. What CM does is to make sure that people do not sink as deeply into the depression phase and that moving along the curve does not take as long. The curve however cannot be avoided. It

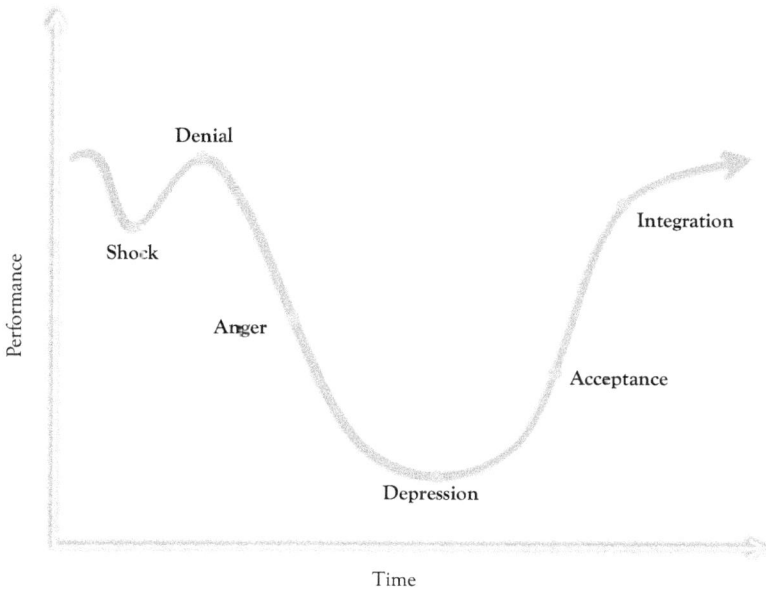

Figure 2.1 The emotional change curve by Kübler-Ross (2003)

Source: Own illustration

results in a central statement about CM: The time factor is significant in change. Sentences like "change is the real constant" do not change the fact that people need time to accept change. The change curve also teaches that different reactions in the different phases are helpful and normal. Those who are in the denial phase need something different from those in the acceptance phase. Good CM always observes and considers the phase in which affected employees find themselves.

Systemic Change Management

CM usually looks at the impact that some change has on people. Systemic CM looks further and deeper. Influenced by systemic therapy and systemic communication theories, systemic CM assumes that one must not look at change in isolation, but deeper into the causes and consequences of change as well as into the affected organization and its environment. Creating new leadership structures, for example, can have a profound impact on individual employees who can express themselves privately.

Even if there are only changes in one department, the neighboring departments and the larger system should be included as well.

Linear Versus Circular

From a Design Thinking approach, we have learned how important iterative processes are. The associated approach is often contrary to many common processes, at least those that occur in large corporations. The latter often want to capture and tame changes, pack them into a project plan, and work on them. Human behavior, however, is not always linear-compliant, but circular-disagreeing. Particularly in change programs, those affected do not always behave predictably rationally, but rather unpredictably emotionally. This means, for example, that those affected by change do not even go through the "valley of tears" in the change curve and then look cheerfully into the future, but can certainly fall back into depression. Anyone who has ever had to deal with serious illness or with people who underwent a deep loss experience will know what is meant. Circular CM expects that not everything will go according to plan, and that intervention steps have to be adapted, abandoned, or reinvented. Likewise, it is often about a simultaneity of interventions. Not everything can be processed linearly.

CM and PM

Classical Project Management (PM) therefore sometimes has its problems with CM. The strength of PM is precisely that it can translate vision into mission, mission into big goals, big goals into small goals, small goals into milestones, and milestones into PM actions that can be accurately tracked for their execution and success.

On the other hand, CM requires a plan with phases and milestones as well. However, this plan should always remain "soft" and customizable. PM and CM should therefore not be seen as opposites, but rather as yin and yang: mutually complementary and common principles of true strength.

Cultural Change

A special form of change is cultural change. After all, culture is the defining element of any organization and, as a sum of values, assumptions, attitudes, beliefs, and the "way-of-doing," it is particularly resistant to change. In our experience, cultural change is possible if, just like any other change, it is viewed in a structured way. The MIC model that I present in this book offers itself here as a transformative cultural change approach. However, a culture is not changed as an office move which can be decided in one week and implemented in the next. Culture is normative and resistant. It is the strength of culture. Nevertheless, it is possible to change it, as we will see from different examples.

Leading Change

John Kotter's "Leading Change" is an excellent description of the elementary dimensions of each change. In MIC, the leadership component of change is part of mindset formation. Leading a change correctly is elemental and will therefore be treated as such.

CHAPTER 3

Mindset

The What—Sensitize for Change

More often than one might believe, in corporate context, it is not clear what the change is exactly. In particular, many project managers think in a goal-oriented but not person-oriented way, as they are usually measured by the achievement of goals and their milestones. Person-oriented project management will ask itself the question at any time of the project: Who exactly is affected by the change? Also, how can we help the person or group of people to go through the emotional change curve and change behavior? Of course, the change manager must also ensure that the foundations of good project management are in place that there is a clear project plan, the project framework is described, the roles are clear, stakeholders are analyzed and influencing strategies are designed, and communication is planned and done correctly.

All people affected by change will have a certain mindset to change long before they even understand what it is all about. This predisposing mindset is influenced by a variety of criteria: the personality (history), previous experience (evaluation), capacity for change (limitation), and the environment (culture). People react differently to change. Some find it easier to change than others because of personal life experiences.

Case Study

Max made a very open impression on me. As the son of an ambassador, he was used to approaching people, asking friendly questions, and creating rapport. Until the age of 20, he had lived in 10 different locations around the world—on three continents—and for no more than two years. We talked about the feeling of being at home and about willingness to change. As for change, he was surprisingly resistant. He had done his complete business administration studies in one place. Of course, he was happy to be "at home" in different places around the world and to have friends there. On the other hand, his personality was characterized by the fact that he apparently wanted stability in his life: For 8 years, the 30-year-old had dated his girlfriend, and for 12 years he lived in the same place. Had his employer asked him to accept a different position in another country, he would have had to think carefully over a period of time about it.

People are predisposed to change based on personal experience. This means that there is a different starting point for each person. The time it takes a person to accept a change also varies according to this predisposition.

One particular way in which personality is influenced in terms of change is prior experience with change. These past experiences mean that change is assessed in advance without its initial implications being known. Such prior experiences can affect the future handling of change both in a positive and negative sense. If the change experience was rather negative, the initial makeup will also be more resistant to change, and vice versa.

Case Study

Over time, there have been countless programs in one business unit, all of which should either increase productivity, minimize costs, increase quality, or increase engagement. Most of these programs have been praised and successfully sold by the respective departments. When people started talking to each other, however, reservations arose: "just another program," according to the motto: do not pay so much attention, play the game, pretend to participate, and wait a year—until the program is over. When it came to just over 2 years and to another program of efficiency increase, you could observe this reaction world-wide. In diagnostics, however, this organizational predisposition was recognized in such a way that it could be proactively addressed.

If people already have had a negative experience with a project, it is important to analyze the mindset well and to expect that there will be (silent) resistance in the future.

In a changing environment, another variant of predisposing mindset can emerge: limited change capacity. Even the most modest man needs a certain amount of stability. Children growing up in an unstable environment have a hard time finding their way. Those who do not experience continuity and stability are literally torn from their feet and unable to survive. For me, it became clear in the face of the biggest change in my life when I left priesthood. Priesthood is not a profession like any other. It is a life form (among other things through celibacy). For example, I never had to save money, naturally had my social environment in church, and had a job I was studying for (theology). Taking the step to give up this job and its civil service such as security was tough. It took long and was well prepared. I had considered which (other) job may fit me and how I could prepare for it. The choice was for the profession of consultant, manager, and coach, and so I started with a management consultancy. In addition to the change in profession came the vocation and way of life. A move was added with and the loss of almost the entire social environment. So I asked myself, "What's left in the face of this radical change? You start at zero, have no friends, you live alone, you must and can reinvent your life." As an avid mountaineer and skier who had spent many weeks in the mountains year after year, I decided to go to the south of Germany to draw close to there—the love of the mountains being the only guarantor of narrow continuity in an experience of massive discontinuity. Every weekend, I spent in the mountains and the pure sight of their height during evening walks gave me comfort, hope, and confidence to master this difficult change.

But there is a limit to digesting change. Man is not as changeable as the words attributed to Charles Darwin, but probably not by him suggests: "It is not the strongest of the species that survives, nor the most intelligent that survives It is the one that is most adaptable to change." Yes, man can adapt to different life situations, can live without eating, drinking, and sleeping, can survive at minus 40 or plus 40 degrees, could be on the moon or settle down on Mars, order new glasses from the optician every year or change his wardrobe every day. Man will however always need stability and continuity, at least in some areas of his life. If there is a lot of change in companies, the person concerned usually still has his or her own private stability (home, family, friends, hobbies, etc.). Nevertheless, frequent changes occurring within a company can cement increased employee resistance to change.[1]

Case Study

During a restructuring, we measured this change capacity and then interpreted the implementation strategy: Countries with more change impact from other change projects were initially spared, while others that had less change at that moment were more open to the change program. One criterion that helps to successfully implement change is to become aware of change capacity or to measure it in advance.

In addition to personal history, the previous experience, and the limited capacity for change, yet another element shapes the mindset to change, the environment in which one lives, work colleagues, friends, acquaintances, structures, in short, culture. In hierarchical structures, for example, it will be more difficult to implement democratic decision-making patterns than in companies with flat hierarchies. In an environment of commitment, excitement, and passion, change is absorbed differently than in a negative culture of criticism, where the negative is sought to affirm to in a "self-fulfilling prophecy." Making decisions, how to work together, how to distribute work in the first place, how to measure and report on success are all culture-creating traits that shape the mindset and can generate greater or lesser resistance to change. Currently, many companies are trying to become more agile, which usually means quick decisions, a flat hierarchy, and high decision-making authority (empowerment). This procedure however is diametrically opposed to many old corporate cultures, especially when it requires many licenses for decisions that affect different levels of hierarchical management and thus keep decision-making authority within narrow limits at respective other levels. This is the case, for example, in a company where the CEO needs to approve

---

[1] Cf. also Axel Koch: Change mich am Arsch. Wie Unternehmen ihre Mitarbeiter und sich selbst kaputt verändern. Berlin 2017.

any job placement, even that of trainees, in HR. One can imagine that the recruitment process is extremely slow and that the HR executives do not feel empowered and motivated.

An environmental and cultural analysis is therefore advisable in every change project, especially at the beginning. With regard to the initial mindset, there are two typical reactions or behaviors: being unaware (passive) or denying (active). In the first reaction, one may already have heard about change but may not be aware of its size or impact. In the second reaction, one simply rejects it. This reaction should not be confused with deep resistance. It is either more superficial "It won't be so bad," "It will probably not affect me," or "Who knows if anything will really happen."

Therefore, in the first phase of any change, it is extremely important to create awareness of the change as such and to make clear why it is important. This happens primarily through sober, fact-driven, perpetuating communication. 3-C-Communication is clear, consistent, and comprehensive (Figure 3.1).

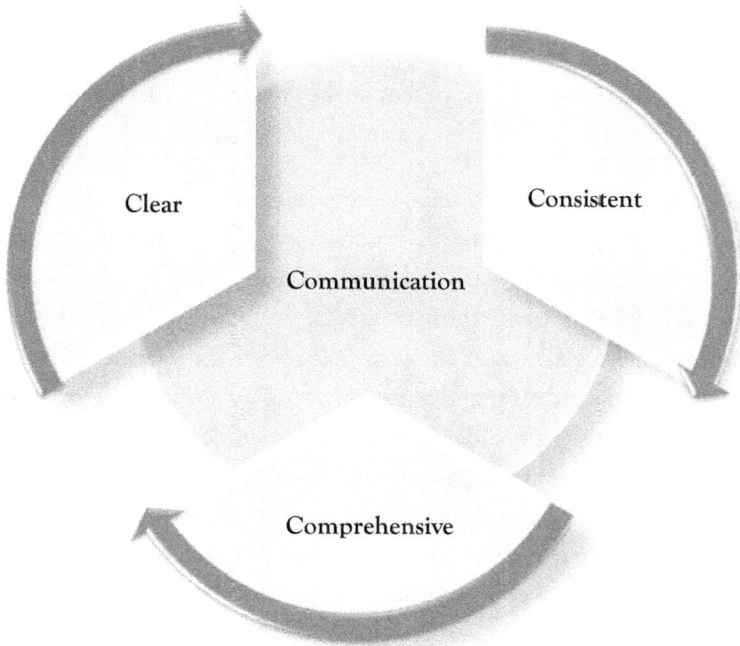

Figure 3.1 *The 3-C-Communication*

Clear communication impresses through its simplicity. If you cannot summarize the change in one sentence, you should think again. Instead of illuminating the change for a long time from different perspectives, the main features should be worked out.

Toolbox

3-C-Communication: Clear, Consistent, Comprehensive

Good change communication is clear, consistent, and comprehensive.

Then the message should be consistent. Nothing is more damaging than "mixed messages" about the change. Whichever channels are used, the message may have different densities but it should not be contradictory.

Finally, communication should be as comprehensive as possible. This means that it covers all areas that have to do with the change and at the same time it delimits what is no longer part of the project.

Toolbox

One-Sentence Statement

One sentence describes the content of the change. The decisive factor is the process that leads to this statement.

A method to generate the one-sentence statement could be as follows. The project team and executives get together in small groups and the understanding of the project is described in one sentence. There may also be two sentences; no tapeworm sentences, but approximately 20-word sentences. Then the sentences are juxtaposed and checked for matches and differences. Both verbatim and analogous matches are specially marked. Finally, one addresses the differences and tries to understand, discuss, and clarify them. The creation of the one-sentence statement is a performative process. It is not just about the result, but also about the evolution of the statement. Often, different understandings and priorities are revealed. Employees are sensitive to communications that keep silent about the true cause of change. For example, when it comes to increasing efficiency through staff cuts, but communicating that change brings only positive things for the company creates a credibility problem that adversely affects people's willingness to change. If certain things are unclear at the beginning of the change, they should be named as well, rather than the team pretend that they know everything.

In addition to the one-sentence statement, it is also possible to explicitly describe what is in scope and out of scope; what is the exact project assignment; which groups of stakeholders does it relate to (which not); which countries are affected? (which not); and so on. Sometimes projects tend to grow in size. Examples of this would be although the new IT was intended only for purchasing, it should now be introduced in production; although only selected countries in Europe were "in scope," Asia is also added now; and so on. The project's inherent tendency to grow bigger can be counteracted by the tool "in or out." For example, when restructuring, it may be helpful to understand which departments, countries, or functions are not affected. If this changes in the course of the change, it is then a deliberate decision that is also communicated as such.

Toolbox

In or Out

All elements that belong to the change are listed within a box, those that do not belong outside the box, and those that need to be discussed are placed on the box's frame.

A 3-C-Communication is important in every phase of the change and can also be gradually adapted. Especially in the first phase, when it comes to raising awareness of the change and making it clear that the change is bound to happen, it is necessary to emphasize the message over and over again.

It was impressive to see in a large change program the commitment a CEO continuously placed on the same message of a new leadership system in different contexts. The bigger the company, the more frequently and in different channels such a message has to be communicated.

As the change progresses, people usually experience another emotional reaction: The more they get out of their comfort zone, the stronger the resistance becomes. This can vary greatly depending on personality type. Not everyone will explicitly tell his leader why change is unacceptable.

Rather, silence in the woods is observed; employees start to update their profile on Linked-In and consider whether they should leave the company. People in this phase do not necessarily need more information or the factual representation of all the positive reasons for change, but rather empathetic managers, employees, and colleagues to whom they can address their questions, criticisms, and possibly bad moods.

In our experience, focus groups are a particularly suitable tool for people in this phase: On the one hand, employees are offered a protected framework in which they can speak out and on the other hand, the methodology helps them to go one step further using the "what if" tool that we will talk about later.

Toolbox

Focus Groups

Horizontally and vertically mixed groups (different hierarchical levels and different attitudes to change) describe their loss experience and formulate possible positive influences of the change.

Who has a role in the change program and what kind of responsibility? Answering this question is particularly beneficial for the project team. When project teams are put together from different functions with people who have never worked together, it results in group-dynamic challenges. Tuckman's phase model is certainly helpful in understanding the stages that each team goes through. From our experience, however, it is helpful to be clear about and agree on the goal, the different roles, and team-internal processes from the beginning.

Toolbox

Team-Building

Clarify goals, processes, and roles.

If change management is defined as the art of guiding people through the emotional change curve so that as many affected people overcome resistance as quickly as possible, adopt a new way of behaving, and thus are able to effectively fulfill their tasks again, the first and most important step is to find out who is affected by and who can influence the change.

Analysis of the Stakeholders

Stakeholder analysis begins with the listing of all stakeholders or stakeholder groups. Some of the stakeholders can belong to both groups: those who are affected by change and those who can influence it. This list of stakeholders is important from two perspectives. First, it helps to avoid forgetting an important group. In some change projects, it only became apparent in the course of the project that there were unforeseen obstacles, because one did not have the affected people in mind and therefore did not manage them. Getting to grips with who is affected by change and in what way helps to avoid this. On the other hand, stakeholder management stems from the development of influencing strategies. Listing or depicting dependencies and their impact on those affected is the first step in developing a strategy for how people can best be managed.

Excursus: Influence Yes or No?

Influencing may have a negative connotation for some. It sounds like manipulation, which means an influence that bypasses the freedom of man or has a negative moral impact, such as when people are purposefully deceived about something. Nobody wants to be manipulated in this sense and every change manager has to be aware of his responsibility when it comes to influence. If, for example, the idea is to manipulate people who lose their job due to a restructuring so that they deliberately remain in the dark until the day of termination, it is morally questionable. Transparency and honesty are certainly better guides.

On the other hand, we know from sales and communication psychology how much we are constantly influenced ourselves and influence others. Which product is on the shelf, which music is playing in the background, which advertising we are confronted with are often the result of a profound psychological influencing strategy.

Strictly speaking, every communication is a form of influence. When I move a person to listen to me, I influence him. The axiom of Watzlawick: "One cannot not communicate." I would expand to "One cannot not influence." In this sense, a conscious, morally justified, *active* influencing and influencing strategy is to be preferred to a passive, possibly negative, and uncontrollable influence. Take the relationship with our supervisors or customers. Forgoing an active influence could mean that others influence the boss or the client (because bias always happens), and that it creates an unfavorable picture of our performance or our product. Active involvement can help us present ourselves or our product in such a way that it helps the relationship with the supervisor or the customer so that our performance or product marketing is conducive. One can also see in this example the possibility of negative manipulation: If the presentation of my accomplishment with which I want to influence the supervisor, or the representation of the product with which I want to advertise customers, is only half true or even a lie, I try to manipulate in a negative sense. In change management courses, there are always lively discussions about this topic. The reason lies from a philosophical perspective in the freedom of the will, which we (have to) defend. The extent to which freedom is really given, how much we are influenced by our childhood, the environment, other people, and so on is currently being discussed in philosophy and theology. This cannot be done at this point. With regard to influencing strategies in change management, the only thing that matters to me is the following:

- Not considering any influencing strategy is in itself an influence. So, according to Watzlawick's axiom, one should rather actively and consciously influence as passively and unconsciously.
- Of course, influencing strategies respect fundamental moral insights like free will or the orientation of the strategy on the fundamentally good for all concerned.

The list of stakeholders is the prerequisite for carrying out an analysis. This has three main impact directions:

- The measurement of resistance or support for the change
- Reasons for rejection and possible arguments of support
- Influencing strategies.

How is a stakeholder analysis carried out in practice? In principle, the project team discusses individuals and groups of people along the three main elements mentioned earlier. Subjective opinions complement each other and lead—deliberately—to discussions of concrete examples, such as why Mr. Miller will probably show a particularly great resistance to the change and Mrs. Smith—presumably—is more inclined to support the change. It is important in the discussion to base assumptions on the most objective observations possible. Nevertheless, for the whole analysis, these are always assumptions that need to be validated in conversations or further observations. Our experience confirms that assumptions are usually correct, especially if the project team consists of well-connected, accessible, communicatively competent, and emotionally intelligent change managers (Table 3.1).

Table 3.1 Stakeholder analysis

Stakeholder	Measurement of resistance	Reasons (personal, political, cultural)	WIIFM	Visualization of the system	Influencing strategy

Measuring resistance or supporting change can be done using a simple numerical scale (e.g., high resistance—medium resistance—no resistance/no support—careful support—proactive support). This gives a first indication of whether critical stakeholders are rated differently or rather similarly and what the reasons for their resistance or support could be.

Then, for each stakeholder, possible reasons for the rejection and possible arguments for support are collected. Why someone does not support a change can have many reasons, from personal to political/cultural. Personal reasons can be based, on the one hand, on personality as such—some people are more resistant, others more innovative—and on the degree of change, which is expected of a person. Take for example a simple change of work processes compared with a massive intervention in life such as a move or a completely new working environment. Political reasons for resistance can arise through loss of power, responsibility or freedom, cultural through drastic changes in culture ("in our case it is …"). For example, when we introduced new performance measurement systems, we saw that there is often an intertwining of the three root causes. Achieving transparency and discussing things together can stand against personal experience and trigger fears that performance is no longer sufficient. From a political perspective, resistance may be due to the loss of power within the sphere of influence for individuals and, finally, from a cultural perspective, it may mean that the current culture is very hierarchical and does not support discussion of continuous improvement per se.

However, any change can also include opportunities for development or new perspectives, which are sometimes not so obvious at the beginning, especially if those involved still oppose the change. It is worthwhile brainstorming for or with the affected stakeholder group to discover whether the change also has positive opportunities. It is about creating what is called WIIFM (What's in it for me). A mistake that is often made is that little is considered from a stakeholder perspective, which is very important. We will come back to the WIIFM later.

Case Study

In one project, the efficiency gains resulting from a modified performance system were not necessarily positive for the end user. In this particular project, however, we were able to work out a WIIFM as the employee obtained a better structure of his everyday work through the new performance system. This WIIFM cleared up chaos and ignorance as to whether what the employees did was actually correct, which had created a basic dissatisfaction in the past.

After a basic assessment as well as reasons for rejection or WIIFM has been worked out for all or at least the most important stakeholder groups, a systemic landscape emerges from which influencing strategies can be derived. For this, it helps to visualize the system of industrial relations. This not only includes departmental structures and reporting lines but also takes into account necessary or voluntary cooperation of different teams, departments, and business units as well as (known) personal relationships. A mindmap-like visualization, for example, using the Stakeholdermap method from Design Thinking, helps to understand who can help who to go through the emotional curve of change and adapt behavior. Both previously defined reasons for refusal and the WIIFM can be addressed here and have a positive effect on communication. What has proven to be particularly helpful is the identification of opinion leaders, who, by their very nature, have a great impact on others and therefore influence them—whether they are against or for change.

How do you find out who is the opinion leader within a group? Relationships are often uncovered directly through conversations or observations. Active surveys can also contribute to this. In practice, questions include "What do you think, who is accepted by most of your department?," "Who speaks the most for your group?," "Who is the most important person to support the change, so that others will follow?"

A stakeholder analysis is dynamic. According to the emotional reaction to change, attitudes of individuals can change several times or assumptions may not be confirmed. That is why it is even more important never to rest on the findings of the analysis, but to consider them with reservation. With every change, however, an in-depth look at the "what" is crucial. The change project as such must be well managed in content, scope, team, and stakeholders. Above all, one question must be clarified, namely "Why do I have to change?"

The Why—Wishes and Needs

Parents know this question only too well. If you ask children to do or leave something, to show a change in their behavior—and nothing else changes—they will usually want a rationale:
"Why?"

There are innumerable examples in everyday life that answering the why question is essential for a successful change. Among other things, it provides information on motivation for a pending change. I am extrinsically motivated when I feel the need for change from the outside, and intrinsically when I want to change myself or because of my own knowledge of a change.

The extrinsically motivated cause may arise after a doctor's visit, if the patient is told that a change in diet is necessary to prevent coronary heart disease. In business, a need for change is often communicated from the top: This change is necessary because we otherwise lose revenue, lose market share, customer satisfaction decreases, and so on. Although this type of communication is important, it remains ultimately questionable whether for the individual employee provides sufficient justification for the change, which is strong enough to trigger a change of mindset through extrinsic motivation.

Case Study

Workplace reorganization centralized printers. The reason: "We become leaner and reduce costs." This was not necessarily convincing or motivating for the employees. The need to change—in this case, leaving the office for each print and fetching the printed paper from the central printer—was not shared on a personal level. It could be said sarcastically that it is not necessary—the idea being that employees follow the new process and costs are reduced. It is exactly what happened. There were long queues at the printer, a lot of time was lost through chatting at the printer, prints were not bundled, but individually commissioned—all in all, productivity fell significantly. The people responsible for this change then looked for a common reason, on the one hand at a factual level, that is, how the process could be better managed, and on the other hand, what were the positive effects for the new central printer. Here was a strong argument that exercise in the workplace is fundamentally positive and beneficial to health. Developing a shared WIIFM—and thus sufficient motivation—helped to see change positive, while at the same time increasing efficiency by lowering printing costs and making the small talk a normal one.

More important, however, is to promote intrinsic motivation. It is not insignificant and at the same time not easy. Not insignificant is because in the long run only intrinsic motivation sticks. Not easy is because new patterns of behavior must be practiced, which must prevail against often years of old patterns. Studies have shown, for example, that even patients who have been named one of the strongest intrinsically motivated *Why*, namely to extend life, only permanently changed their behavior to a certain extent.

An intrinsic motivation to change behavior can develop in some cases by itself and it can then be promoted from the outside accordingly. If I have been dissatisfied with my boss for some time and am therefore thinking about changing jobs, I am intrinsically motivated to change. If a restructuring of the company gives me a new manager, I will almost certainly support and motivate this change.

Assisting in the emergence of intrinsic motivation can be a "away-from-and-toward" movement in terms of individual attitudes. First of all, we should consider why an old working environment, old habits, and old patterns of behavior are no longer suitable or attractive and the person concerned wants to leave them (= "away from"). On the other hand, we must define what is so attractive in the new work environment, new habits, or new behavioral patterns to encourage the person concerned to go there (= "toward"). The classical example of a desire to change, namely to quit smoking, shows that often works only on the away from motivation (harmful, expensive, odor, etc.), but not on an attractive image of the future (more efficient, more money for other more worthwhile activities, goods, or the like), leads to failure. In the absence of this, the smoking positives are easily recaptured (relaxation, social, simple habit). To develop a strong *Why*, it is necessary to make the path-of-motivation concrete (what exactly does the damage to health mean, how much money do you save, when are the odor receptors regenerated to make new olfactory experiences?). This helps develop own motivation (how do you rebuild your health, what do you do with the money saved, how do you build other social relationships, what do you do to relax, etc.) (Figure 3.2).

The trigger of a path of motivation is also called a "burning platform" in change management. Imagine standing on an oil platform in the wild-moving ocean with a fire behind you and foaming waves beneath. The more the fire spreads, the greater the pressure or the need for something to change. Jumping 30 meters into the ocean depths, without knowing what awaits you, or whether the chosen future will really be better than the threatened past. This is a scenario that makes the ultimate goal clear: To change even if the future does not (yet) seem particularly convincing, we need the absolute conviction that the past no longer works. I am aware of a few biographies in which those affected could only take a drastic step of change in their lives when a "burning platform" had been created for them. A typical statement in this context is "I just had to make this step of change—even though it was difficult and a lot of things held me back."

How Is It Possible to Build a "Burning Platform"?

First of all, the various stakeholder groups are examined by the question of which reasons might motivate them to change. We have already introduced the WIIFM, which can give some clues as to the reasons that motivate change. Arguments can be formulated even more precisely if you sort them by these two questions:

- What is at stake if I do not change?
- What options do I have if I change?

Negative Consequences of the Status Quo

The status quo usually is nothing frightening at first; otherwise, you would immediately change something. At this point, it is therefore a question of consciously working out possible negative consequences of the status

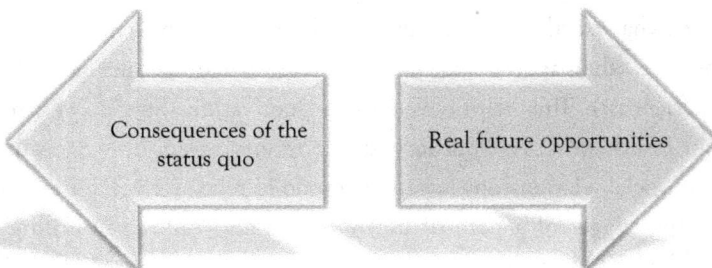

Figure 3.2 *Away-from-and-toward motivation*

quo and then communicating. In other words, the risks of sticking to the status quo need to be understood. Countless examples of companies that have gone down or become meaningless discuss this connection: The status quo was so secure and consequently risk averse that there was no need for change. Those companies that at some point in their history have the realistic consequences, if everything stays as it is, they have been able to induce change in time.

In describing the status quo, art consists in discussing for each stakeholder the realistic consequences that affect it. Sometimes these consequences are not obvious from the outset and need to be sought consciously, but sometimes they are obvious. Arguments, such as "If we do not change, we lose market share," which like to be led by higher levels of leadership, are not really a "burning platform" to lower-level employees in the hierarchy. Even the accompanying standard argument "Then you will lose your job!" does not automatically cause a strong motivation for change, because there are often signs of wear and tear. Too often programs have been announced with such importance, which then fizzled out as the laxity of the structures and their employees have prevailed in the long run.

Case Study

An IT implementation project identified "the consequence of the status quo" in that employees could only evolve if they were involved in the project. Not embarking on this learning journey would mean employees lose touch. This argument was also convincing: To continue blocking the change and sticking to the status quo would mean not only learning nothing new but also losing the connection with the other colleagues and the company in the long term. This argument was so strong that it was instrumental in creating the "burning platform."

Real Future Opportunities

What are the positive opportunities for me, *if* I change myself? On the one hand, development and formulation of this line of reasoning supports change. On the other hand, close attention must be paid to future opportunities being:

- realistic

- concrete
- stakeholder-specific.

Future opportunities are realistic if the stakeholder gets a positive impression that the future is better for him than the present. They are concrete if their occurrence in the future is probable and feasible. They are stakeholder-specific if the stakeholder or the stakeholder group feels addressed by the future (toward motivation). All three characteristics should be addressed together and not completely separately.

Case Study

An employee is offered a promotion which, however, requires relocation. Why should accepting this offer be attractive for him and his family? The elaboration of actual opportunities showed that he was better able to indulge in his hobby: Being a semi-professional musician, live in a new city where his children and his partner had better options for further development and live in a city which had "Nice-to-live-in" places.

The Where — The Target State

Neurobiology has given us interesting insights. The brain can hardly differentiate between real and fictitious happenings. Conceptual ideas and real experiences are equated by the brain (to a great extent).

This has a fundamental consequence for change management: If an emotionally appealing vision of the future is communicated, the future already starts to become real in the minds of the participants. There are impressive visions of the future from famous personalities such as the line "I have a dream," from the speech that Martin Luther King gave in 1963 in Washington, in which he outlined overcoming racial segregation.

I have a dream that one day this nation will rise up and live out the true meaning of its creed: "We hold these truths to be self-evident: that all men are created equal."

> I have a dream that one day on the red hills of Georgia the sons
> of former slaves and the sons of former slave owners will be able to sit
> down together at a table of brotherhood.
>
> I have a dream that one day even the state of Mississippi, a state
> sweltering with the heat of injustice and sweltering with the heat of
> oppression, will be transformed into an oasis of freedom and justice.
>
> I have a dream that my four little children will one day live in a
> nation where they will not be judged by the colour of their skin, but
> by the content of their character.
>
> I have a dream today!
>
> Martin Luther King, 1963[2]

The peculiar thing about this vision of the future is that King speaks less of cold facts and figures; rather, he builds emotionally appealing images, which moves the listeners and thus builds up force for the future.

Such future visions, communicated and received in this manner, are rare. Rather, many people follow the dictum of the late former chancellor Helmut Schmidt: "Those who have visions[3] should go to the doctor." The appeal to be realistic resonates with people, because several visions of the future are too unrealistic, less appealing, and thus not really motivating and consequently illusory or even misleading, or rather, counterproductive.

So, the development of the "to-be" (both the intended "prospective" as well as of the "target state") and its communication must therefore be forward-looking, emotionally appealing, and realistic.

Every change promises a future, which is better than the present. This promise correlates with a deep human yearning that tomorrow will be better than today. Therefore, a good vision of the future will describe this "better tomorrow" in detail. The important thing here is that this vision does not just consist of facts and figures, but also it should stir emotions. It achieves that by describing in images and narratives, *how* the future will look. In some workshops, participants select unrealistic descriptions in the vision exercise, such as "at the sorter, we first drink coffee for an hour

---

[2] Source: https://americanrhetoric.com/speeches/mlkihaveadream.htm (accessed on December 2018).

[3] The German meaning of vision is hallucination as well.

in order to subsequently go to the gym." The instruction for this change step thus gives a realistic description of the target state which simultaneously touches and convinces.

Case Study

People control processes or processes control people. Often enough, they are only described soberly, almost mechanically, without considering the human factor. In case of a major cultural change within an organization, new processes have been mapped and there has been an exact description as to what that meant for the people concerned and their new behavior. The vision of change described the new processes from the human perspective, made them appealing, and helped employees identify with them. This way, the nonexistent, planned reality has been created in advance which helped employees modify their behavior according to the future state.

How Does Vision Development Look from a Practical Perspective?

In a workshop format, participants are invited to describe the target state in various categories, with emphasis on target attainment, data, process, organizational, performance, and behavioral descriptions. To address not just the prefrontal cortex, the base of rationality in the brain, but also the limbic system, particularly the Amygdala as the base control of emotion,[4] it is recommended that the future state is depicted, both using word and text as well as images, color, and emotion.

Toolbox

What-If Tool

In the workshop format, employees describe the future, in terms of how it could look after the cultural change, particularly from a behavioral and quality perspective.

---

[4] Also see https://thoughtco.com/limbic-system-anatomy-373200 (accessed September 23, 2019).

This development process, in which the possible future state is described, can already induce change. Over and above that, vision development can also be used to identify required change milestones. At the behavioral level it can be used to define what behaviors can be continued, should be stopped, and should be started: The so-called SCS tool (start, continue, stop) describes at the behavioral level how employees approach the target state. For example, if it concerns a better performing team and the target state describes processes and how work can be done together to add value, then the SCS tool could look like this:

- **Start**—conduct a conversation each day with each colleague
  - Discuss each project with a colleague as a "buddy"
- **Continue**—hold weekly calls
  - Meet a colleague for dinner twice a week
- **Stop**—Implement projects single-handedly
  - Inform colleagues about a project only after kickoff

It is important to use concrete formulations as well as SMART (specific, measurable, attainable, realistic, time-bound) goals, verifiable and observable behavior, which is demanded and called for by the sponsor. If "Start" states "be nicer" or "apply the new process," it will not create any behavioral change.

Toolbox

SCS Tool

- Start: Which behavior should be started to achieve the vision?
- Continue: Which behavior should be continued to achieve the vision?
- Stop: Which behavior should be stopped to achieve the vision?

The so-called change story is a different product or tool. This is particularly helpful when dealing with major changes because it specifically deals with and visualizes the *What* and *Why*. It states what was good in the past and therefore what may also be appreciated about it. In the same way, shortcomings and changes are pointed out, which have led to old behaviors not being continued any more ("burning platform").

Toolbox

Change Story

The history of change is visualized taking the following questions into consideration:
- What was the past like?
- What was good and may therefore be appreciated?
- What should change and why?
- What does the future look like?
- How can each person contribute toward a positive future?
- What does leadership promise and what does it expect?
- What are the next steps?

Driving the entire change, leadership behavior is pivotal. In the following section, we will examine what management expects in this context.

The Leadership—The Role Model Function (Role Modeling)

If in a company one asks what the decisive factor is for successful change, the answer will almost always be "leadership." This usually means that top executives in a company, regardless of how strong or less strong it is built hierarchically, are decisive for the success of change. Along the MIC methodology, it appears that the role of an executive alone is not crucial but still important for the success of any change project. Change projects can be started and can also succeed initially even without explicit support from the top. To become part of the culture however, the support and moreover role model function of executives (leadership sponsorship) are inalienable.

Case Study
One example is the implementation of the "Search inside yourself" method in a Dax30 company. Change began with a few employees,

who lived the method of mindfulness and had successfully completed internal training. After numerous other employees had taken part in the training and had implemented it in their daily routine, it was down to top executives to deal with the topic in greater detail and to support the further rollout of change.

As a rule, active leadership is necessary from the outset for future action (role modeling), to motivate, to communicate, and to ensure implementation of all MIC elements.

Role Modeling

Employees are very sensitive to the consistency between word and action from their leaders, also due to relevant lessons learned. Promises may have been made very often, but not kept, or messages sugar-coated so that it became unclear what the actual message was behind the official communication. With respect to any change, people concerned will first evaluate the action or behavior of the conveyor of the message before the message itself. If executives try to change their behavior in the desired direction, but are not authentic it will be in vain. Authenticity is decisive. To clarify it, we will first ask the following basic question:

What makes the role model function so challenging and what can executives do to be perceived as a role model?

For historic reasons, the direct translation of the English word "Leader" (Führer) is rarely used in German. Normally, it refers to executives. An executive is first an impersonal designation and describes a profession or an activity. In the sense of "Leader," executive means a person with his own needs, injuries, ideas, desires, and traits. Thus, the executive being a role model is not the aspiration of a neutral person, an impersonal force, but the challenge for a tangible person to demonstrate certain behaviors. As these behaviors usually do not coincide automatically with the habitual or preferred behaviors of an executive, a behavioral change is required, which occurs neither automatically nor without resistance. It is always astonishing when, as with most changes (rightly), the management's role model function is emphasized, but simultaneously there is an impression created that pure appeal is adequate to bring about desired behavior.

Human predisposition regarding change and the fact that all executives are individuals with their own histories and resistances to change is hardly taken seriously at all. Turning executives into role models for change is a not to be underestimated change.

Case Study

An attempt was made to implement the principle of holistic leadership in a large corporation. Every time role models were sought, the same five names came up among 400 executives. They were role models because of their personal character, regardless of the change which was required by the new leadership culture. Coaching and feedback methods were used to work with all the top executives to practice new behaviors. In the process, it could be seen that about 10 percent were willing to learn and the new behaviors were accepted quickly, whereas it was almost impossible for another 10 percent. The majority of 80 percent were more or less ready to learn, but required more time to adopt and assimilate the new behaviors.

One said that

> Basically one can say that the greater the gap from current behaviour for the executives to be covered, the more investment is required for their development, so that they can become role models. The smaller the gap between actual and target behaviour, the easier it is to develop them into role models with respect to new behaviour. In cultural transformations, where executives ought to demonstrate empathetic behaviour, special investment in the behavioural change of management is necessary.

The deciding question here is whether such a behavioral change is possible at all or whether the behavior is similar to character traits: Can training transform an introvert into an extrovert and can a number-oriented person become people-oriented? Research over recent years shows that basic character disposition always remains but profound behavioral change is possible. Chade-Meng Tan (2014) is referred to here as an example through Mindfulness. With the book *Search Inside Yourself* related to mindfulness, he has shown that emotional intelligence is an ability that can be learned.

The main challenge of being a role model is the fact that it often requires a change in personal behavior. Executives are ideally aware of this, however, without knowing how they are supposed to accomplish it. Congruent behavior of executives with respect to change is decisive to successfully implement cultural change in a company. Therefore, activities that help management in adapting its behavior are required.

Before dealing with a corresponding model in detail, we should take a look at the possible resistances with regard to change. These are categorized as personal, political, and cultural.

- **Personal resistances:** Taking into consideration the past, every person deals differently with change; this is due to genetic preconditions, as well as impressions gained during childhood. This can be seen in some examples of social change, for example, technological development. Where a few people ("Innovators") obtain the latest Smartphone right after it is launched on the market, others prefer to wait ("Waiters") and jump on the bandwagon sooner or later, and others get such a technical device years later, or even never ("Resistors"). Age also plays a role, or rather habit in how long a specific behavior has been "practiced." It is easier for people who are used to working on themselves (which is also a habit).

- **Political resistances:** In (higher) management particularly, behavior is influenced by the so-called political circumstances. What a person does, what promotes or hinders a career, and what the support of certain circles facilitates or hinders for a person are not negligible elements of a politically motivated behavioral approach. For example, if my direct superior does not support change, which is supposed to be enforced by top management, I find myself in a stressful environment which requires making an important decision.

- **Cultural resistances:** Both corporate culture as well as country-or region-specific cultures shape disposition with respect to change. Corporate culture as the entirety of values, convictions, and attitudes influences and shapes the behavior of fellows of the culture. This is a major factor of manifestation for resistance. Personal behavioral change "against" the corporate or even local culture is virtually impossible. If, therefore, in a given change, behavioral change is necessary and the new behavior is contrary to the behavior of the present culture, cultural topics need to be explicitly worked on, or separate initiatives must be drafted which support the change.

Whatever the reason for resistance, the main question is how behavioral changes or resistance can be overcome, so that executives set an example for "exemplary" new behavior. Here again, the MIC model serves with the following main questions:

- What is the new required role model behavior? Which elements support this new attitude? (M)
- Which structural elements support the role model behavior and make the old behavior impossible? (I)
- What are the abilities that the executives need in order to portray the new behavior? (C)

Motivating Leadership

In his book *Mythos Motivation – Wege aus einer Sackgasse*[5] (Motivation Myth—Away from a dead end), Reinhard K. Sprenger challenges incentive systems as motivation control. Motivating people is not just a question of bonus, in fact Sprenger says that praising can be demotivating in the long run. He pleads that intrinsic motivation be encouraged, wherein companies lay down the correct framework conditions. The main task of executives must be to prevent demotivation so that people are encouraged and challenged. If one takes a closer look at the corporate landscape, and not just in Germany, the impression quickly arises that the reception of

---

[5] Reinhard K. 2010. *Sprenger: Mythos Motivation—Wege aus einer Sackgasse*. Frankfurt/New York

this groundbreaking book is still pending. Most managers in our projects understand motivation to mean praise and remuneration systems, especially bonus payments. Different studies show that monetary incentive systems can even be counterproductive to motivation.[6]

What then is successful in increasing motivation in employees? In addition to the advice by Sprenger (2010), which especially covers agreeing on performances, agreed targets and communication, the three main factors for motivation from our experience, which Daniel Pink[7] mentioned, are: Autonomy, Mastery, and Purpose. Incidentally, Pink also showed that extrinsic motivation is a lot less effective than intrinsic.

- **Autonomy:** An important factor for personal satisfaction is the perception of whether one's own life is controlled by oneself or by others. A decisive factor of motivation even when working is how to make independent decisions. Zappos has adapted customer service in such a way that employees independently determine when and how they will work—so long as they contribute to the overarching objective, which is to offer the best possible customer service. While an average call center sees an employee turnover of 35 percent, the figure at Zappos was 15 percent in the year 2016.[8] It is therefore the job of executives to provide employees the option of being able to work autonomously. In very standardized work environments, there are areas in which employees can make their own decisions. This perception of self-control affects motivation.
- **Mastery:** Each person has the intrinsic need to progress and to continuously improve their abilities. If employees are enabled to do not just what is required of them, but also to

---

[6] http://harvardbusinessmanager.de/blogs/gehalt-mehr-geld-fuehrt-nicht-zu-mehr-motivation-und-zufriedenheit-a-907448.html (accessed January 1, 2019).
[7] Daniel Pink. *Drive*. Riverhead 2009.
[8] https://retail.emarketer.com/article/zappos-ceo-tony-hsieh-on-holacracy-customer-service-zappos-anything/58e8084eebd4000a54864afc (accessed January 3, 2019).

rise to challenges, an attitude of satisfaction develops, which in turn develops intrinsic motivation.

- **Purpose:** This does not just mean doing something great and important, but the understanding of working toward a greater goal. For example, Google's purpose is not to be the most effective search engine in the world, rather to make information accessible to everybody in the world. No matter what Google employees are working on, they are intrinsically motivated by the guiding principle that their work enables more people to access important information. The purpose of DPDHL is not to transport packages from A to B as fast as possible, but "Connecting people and Improving lives." Worldwide logistics connects people. It is not just sending medicinal products that are dispatched critically and timely, but also improving lives: Many other things from auto suppliers, technology, and retail sector products are also transported. Executives must communicate this purpose and it must remain consistent. If people cannot identify with it, it will not be motivating.

Our experience tells us that Autonomy, Mastery, and Purpose are far more important for lasting motivation as incentive measures or, even less, motivational speeches, which have nothing to do with reality. This change in mindset, far from deliberation "How do I motivate the employees?" (extrinsic) to "How can I create framework conditions which encourage motivation?" (intrinsic), is fundamental. The framework conditions are substantiated by the provision of autonomous choices for decision making and options for personal development as well as the demonstration of a greater purpose. The deciding factor is how the executive communicates these contents.

Leadership and Communication

One often hears the sentence: "One can never communicate enough," which perhaps arouses strong resonance because of the prevailing assumption that there is too little communication. In fact, there is both, a little too much, and too little communication. The question is less quantitative, in terms of the volume of communication, than qualitative, according to what, when, how, and with whom you communicate. Deciding on and preparing the groundwork for communication is a leadership role, which should not be delegated in a hurry.

Communicate with Whom?

Before one asks the "What" question, it is also important from a change management perspective to think of the stakeholder, in this case, the target group for communication. Consider whether it concerns individuals or large groups, management or employees, people who are concerned directly or indirectly. The communication channel will orient itself along this distinction:

- **Individuals or large groups:** Change is usually initiated by management. This implies that individuals (managers) are targeted first and they expand to circles bit by bit. There are however situations in which everybody or at least large groups are communicated to from the beginning. This can also change during the course of a change process. In any case, communication must be consistent; the density of information however is adaptive.

- **Management or employees:** Good communication to management does not consist of just information, but also support options as to how progress of change can be communicated to employees. In a large, global IT change, for example, a monthly conference call is set up for country managers in which the exact progress of change is communicated. It is up to each country to communicate to employees depending on the degree of change.

- **People concerned directly or indirectly:** The manner in which employees are affected by the change influences the communication channel to a great extent. Naturally, there is a wide spectrum between marginal or indirect and detailed with those directly concerned people. It is very helpful to keep track of the degree of involvement so as to determine the mode and depth of communication required. Communication also adapts itself along the emotional change curve. The greater the degree of involvement, the more the emotional reactions will be and the more deliberation as to what is to be communicated and when. The change curve roughly specifies the content and medium: The first phase is mainly concerned with sober facts and background information, whereas in the second, communication should be in dialogue form to provide individuals the chance to address their questions (and emotions). The third phase combines facts and emotions and the fourth phase authorizes those concerned to become communicators themselves.

Along with the question regarding who to communicate to, the question of what is communicated is also deeply connected.

What to Communicate?

Questions which arise through this connection are What is the change?, Why?, Where do we stand now?, and What do we expect from you?

Misunderstandings mainly arise when different messages are given by the same team or by leadership. Here, it is important to clearly define the What of the change at the outset, at best using a one-line statement (see chapter 3.1). Similarly, it is also important to refer to the Why. Even if the reasons for change have to be adapted to stakeholders, it is important to be able to list an overriding reason, which is not restricted to general phrases such as "to remain market leader." The project team will jointly formulate status updates at regular intervals particularly when preparing personal communication. As experience teaches us, there is an increasing amount of inconsistent information as the project progresses, which can be avoided if a joint memo is discussed and is fixed in writing.

When to Communicate?

In many of our change projects, the communication work stream is marked as a continuous element in the project charter. This does not imply that communication should be anytime and anywhere and done indiscriminately. For example, the so-called communication material was dispatched to all locations of the multinational group for implementing a Lean approach: posters, gadgets, figures, pins, and so on. An infinite number of useful or even unnecessary materials were supposed to support communication. The materials were either discarded without being opened or landed in offices without any context. Years later, rather amusing stories were exchanged about this, which demonstrated that communication relevant to instruction and context had neither been started, nor been done at the right time.

The time as to when and what should be communicated is based on the localization of the stakeholder group on the emotional change curve. For example, it hardly makes sense to dive deep into details of benefits of a new IT system straight at the outset. Instead, fundamental questions should be answered as to what it is actually about, what the rough schedule is, and what likely changes will occur. There is no standard reply for the When and the How-often question; rather, there is an indication to bind communication closely to progress specific stakeholders along the emotional change curve.

How to Communicate?

Many immediate e-mails or staff meetings (town halls) are associated with communication but communication channels can vary. For one, there exist direct channels in personal, small and large group meetings, which can vary a lot with respect to time (from brief memo to information day) and with regard to the group size (from individual interviews, staff meetings, and group calls).[9] On the other hand, indirect channels (e-mail, letter, PowerPoint presentation, etc.) have established themselves and have been supplemented in recent years by social media (Apps, Yammer, etc.).

There is no "one-size-fits-all" answer for the question as to when which medium should be selected. Generally speaking, indirect channels are available for large groups and for the so-called background noise,

---

[9]   Google, for example, conducts one call every week in which principally every employee can participate. It is conducted by the company's founders/CEOs.

whereas direct channels are selected during issues and at important times on the emotional change curve.

Leadership Enables MIC

In addition to right communication, leadership has yet another special role. Leadership only enables development of the right mindset and development of the necessary capabilities. In other words, in every change, MIC functions as a compass, which leads the way for the executive and tells him what he must do to make the change successful: Executives must ensure that the correct mindset is established for change, as has been shown earlier. They also need to ensure that the infrastructure elements are adapted. Over and above that, the executives ensure that employees are competent and the right talent is available for achieving the target state.

Before we deal with infrastructure and capability in greater detail, we will turn our attention to two other elements that influence mindset and which support change.

Continuous Improvement and Growth Mindset

As we have seen already, there are different manifestations in perseverance, depending on personality. Nevertheless, many will agree with the view that people want tomorrow to be better than today. Particularly, there is the intrapsychic search for stability and with that an inclination for status quo. But a person also possesses intrinsic motivation to improve himself and his surroundings. The balance between persisting in status quo and inclination to change is characterized differently in people. Leadership in the 21st century must extrapolate this balance for organizations also: What are the constituting elements that remain, in which areas is change a mandate? Large corporations like Kodak or Nokia, who have lost their market leadership in the shortest time, focused more on status quo than on continuous improvement.

This also mentions the *Why*, why there exists a necessity for continuous improvement and why it must be created by an active leadership. The skill here is to combine this extrinsic necessity with intrinsic motivation, that tomorrow will be better than today.

In some of our change projects, we asked our employees what their best (work) day looked like in the past. From this description, we could separate action and behavior patterns, linked to the question as to what must be done to realize this "best day" tomorrow and also the day after tomorrow. This resulted in activities related to continuous improvement. In this manner, a mindset of continuous improvement is induced and supported, which is a catalyst not to be underestimated fundamentally for every change. Organizations, whose culture subsists on continuous improvement, find it easier to adapt to small and major changes.

However, continuous improvement poses a threat: For some employees, the mindset of continuous improvement translates into "I am never good enough." The best way to deal with them is that achievement is celebrated and improvement steps achieved are rewarded.

The mindset of continuous improvement is closely related to the growth mindset. Growth, in this context, is not just understood as a market entry strategy, but as a holistic social concept: Growth means change, and it means passing phases, which—just like in adolescence—are characterized by trying and also failing. The folk wisdom "Stagnation is regression" points out the fact that there can be no further development without growth. Again, in this fundamental sense, growth also means consolidation growth or deepening client relationships or further personal development of employees by training and feedback. The important thing is that this mindset is enshrined in corporate culture by corresponding communication and activities. The TGIF day[10] at Google probably should also be understood in this sense: Employees are encouraged to grow, wherein they generate new ideas, which on their part become projects or even offers that in turn contribute to corporate growth.

Summary

In every change, it is important to clarify the what, why, and where of change.

---

[10] Thanks God, it's Friday: One day of the working week, Friday, is set aside for creative projects.

Then, it means clarifying the role of executives for change and supporting them both in their own role model function as well as in employee communication. Finally, continuous improvement must be made a part of change.

Leadership and Stakeholder Management are, as it were, the core of every change and therefore need more attention.

Similarly, the question still needs to be asked whether the concerned people can do what they are supposed to and whether structural elements support the present condition or can be adapted in such a way that they will pay off in the future. "Infrastructure" as a change enabling element is often underestimated. The different elements of "infrastructure" need to be discovered now and considered with regard to their relevance to change.

CHAPTER 4

Infrastructure

In infrastructure usually, the technical (roads, energy supply, etc.) and the social (health and education system, etc.) are differentiated. In the corporate and change context, infrastructure means all physical and mental elements, which encourage, support, and enhance a behavior. In particular, it includes physical infrastructure such as office environment, and organizational infrastructure elements such as IT, process, assessment, development. Common to all infrastructure elements is that they can include both tangible as well as mental levels, which may also mesh together in parts.

Change includes, for example, monetary behavioral reward for infrastructure. Behavioral reward in this case includes physical elements such as a concrete reward, and also the underlying (invisible) process such as how attained behavior is controlled by a corresponding process.

Infrastructure Enables, Supports, and Develops Behavior Further

Every instance of human behavior in a company is embedded in a physical and mental context. Let us take for example the cooperation in a team. For cooperation to be effective in the first place, the organization of decision and input/output processes as well as other constituting parameters must be available, in addition to a minimum of communication structures. People who, for example, are waiting together in a room are not necessarily a team. Only a common task such as painting a picture and adopting different roles for the same can make them a team. The ensuing discussion as to how, which picture should be created then develops group-dynamic processes in a new team, which either create or hinder the result.

Supporting infrastructure here means the one which encourages desirable behavior and hinders unwanted behavior. Decision-making rules, for example, by selecting the best proposal, can support a specific behavior and target vision, whereas the infrastructure rule of "Everyone does what he wants" can thwart the desired common target vision. Evolving infrastructure is that, which positively challenges the desired behavior, enhances it or takes it to the next level. In this case, it includes coordinating on a common method, which produces the best target vision.

These three infrastructure attributes describe the chronological procedures in the creation of an infrastructure. The first element (enable/encourage) aids in the change context, to become aware of the corresponding infrastructure, the second (support) differentiates between supporting and hindering infrastructure, whereas the third element (enhance) targets further development or implementation of new elements (Table 4.1).

In any case, infrastructure is similar to a framework that enables, strengthens, or hinders concrete behavior. Therefore, it is especially important to adapt infrastructure of a change such that it works toward a specific change.

Physical Infrastructure

Both the building as such, as well as the offices, items of equipment, and the surroundings in general are important infrastructural elements of every change.

Buildings can play an important role in CM or they may also be ignored if they have no influence over direct change. Latter is frequently the case for IT implementations. Nevertheless, this aspect should not be

Table 4.1 *Infrastructure overview: Enable, Support, Enhance (ESE) model*

	Enable	Support	Enhance
Physical infrastructure			
IT infrastructure			
Process infrastructure			
Measurement infrastructure			
Rewarding/ appreciation infrastructure			
Personal development infrastructure			

ignored here. As the office architecture, for example, essentially depends on which preconditions are given in a building: If offices are located in a building from the 1950s or in a transparent multilevel high-rise building, it influences the culture or the self-image of those who work there. The company building also as such influences cultural change. We were able to observe this aspect in several change projects: Relocation to another building can even be a significant aspect of the change, as commuter habits are mainly altered here.

Furthermore, infrastructure of storage units plays a major role for logistics. As part of cultural changes, it is worth here to start with a solid analysis.

Case Study

An employee-engagement-project showed that employees had to suffer from heat in the hall, but management did not want to install any fans as they whirl paper in the air at critical points in the process and could thus be a potential cause of an accident. The common need and hazard analysis was able to cause a changed arrangement of units, which ensured fresh air, and also was able to minimize hazard from paper twirling around the air.

In any case, at the start of each change, it needs to be analyzed as to how the building infrastructure appears, which effect does it have on the change, whether it enables the change, and how a change of the building or within the building supports or even enhances the cultural change.

During restructuring, if offices in the company are part of the change, then infrastructural implications need particular attention. Studies show that team performance improves if the distance between two offices, whose teams are supposed to work together, is reduced. So, to build more agile structures, open-plan offices are introduced especially in companies with longer tradition. However, studies show that open-plan offices do not necessarily lead to higher productivity per se.[1] In our context, "workplace organization" as an infrastructural element of change must be measured

---

[1] For this, see: https://hbr.org/2014/10/workspaces-that-move-people (accessed January 3, 2018).

with regard to its correlation to change: To what extent does the office environment enables the respective change, supports it, and enhances it is the leading question. A few examples should explain this connection.

- **Team cooperation:** Whenever restructuring, reorganizations, or cultural change initiatives concern teams, it is important to examine the infrastructural preconditions with respect to team functionality. Virtual teams usually hold physical meetings only from time to time, but they require a clearly structured virtual team environment. If teams are used to having their main places of work in close proximity to each other, their change affects immediate cooperation and performance. According to ESE logic, in case of changes to places of work, the change manager will first examine the office infrastructure that enables team work, to then present those structures that strengthen and enhance cooperation. Here, infrastructure is not just restricted to the location of the desk or PC. But, its arrangement, just like other communication and process structures, must be reviewed for enabling or preventing good cooperation. If, for example, for reasons of efficiency, network printers are introduced and local office printers are pared, which can help in promoting cooperation between the different departments, as network printers are the new kitchenettes, so to say. Team work can be directly promoted by consciously creating occasions for "collision."[2]
- **Hierarchical silo structures:** Office arrangements reflect the hierarchy, decision-making processes, and the structure of the organization and strengthen the invisible part of infrastructure.

Case Study
In a change process, process improvements and new performance measurement systems from lean management have been introduced. Our department was—as so often happens—only called in when the

---

[2] Ibid.

normal PM could not achieve the desired results. An initial analysis revealed the obvious: The office complex from the 1960s also breathed this culture, which comprised clear instructions and individual tasks, reflected by long corridors with individual offices separated from the aisle by wooden doors, whose doors were also only opened for going to the toilet. The cooperation that lean management required was not supported by infrastructure. This pattern of behavior and attitudes rooted deeply in culture cannot just be overcome by interplay of the MIC aspects. As infrastructural component, the wooden doors were removed or rather replaced by glass doors, team meetings were conducted in separate rooms, which replaced daily work consisting of 90 percent individual work into 50 percent collaboration structure in pleasant rooms specially furnished for that, and so on.

In classical companies, common office situations reflect the classic "command-and-control" culture: "Normal" employees share an office; the secretary is in the room facing the department or division manager, who on his part has the most spacious office with the best view. Companies with less tradition or smaller units and start-ups frequently have only open-plan offices with conference rooms. The picture of Mark Zuckerberg, where he has pitched his mobile workplace in the open-plan office right next to an intern, has become famous.

In the current discussion about agility and flatter hierarchies in particular, infrastructure is currently viewed without the supplementary aspects of mindset and capability. Classic office structures support a specific culture, which can be contextually helpful. In an environment defined by clearly structured processes, decision mechanisms are not to be discussed and high reliability, flat, hierarchy-supporting infrastructures can be counterproductive, whereas a culture of creativity and innovation needs an infrastructure which supports quick decisions and close cooperation across all responsibilities.

- **Digital workplace:** The workplace models discussed as part of digitization suggest, on the one hand, flexibility of the knowledge worker with regard to workplace location (espe-

cially, home office or tele-working job), and on the other
hand it refers to flexible workplaces without a fixed seat ("hot
desks") or open-plan offices.

At this point, it needs to be mentioned once that each office situation
has its own advantages and disadvantages and that the office infrastructure reflects the cooperation, decision, and leadership mechanisms of the
respective organization. If the silo mentality and steep hierarchies need
to be overcome, it will be beneficial to discuss them in the context of a
holistic organization design. Otherwise, there will be frictions that are not
conducive to the respective ambitions for performance.

Equipment

All work equipment, which is affected by the change project or affects it,
plays an enabling, supporting, or enhancing role as physical infrastructural element. The elements belonging to IT or measurement infrastructure should be dealt with separately (see the sections "IT Infrastructure"
and "Measurement Infrastructure").

The so-called white-collar workers (employees in the office and services sector) or knowledge workers[3] usually require only place (desk) for
working, a PC with Internet connection, and a telephone or another
means of communication.[4] For workshops, this particularly includes basic
things such as post-its, flipcharts, and pens. These enabling infrastructural
aids may be considered a matter of course, but they may play an important role in change projects. Thus, they are not to be underestimated, for
example, in team changes, which are supposed to transform employees
from those working according to pure standards and in silos into creative,
theme-oriented groups of employees.

In logistics, on the other hand, in case of the so-called blue-collar
workers there is a myriad of items of equipment, from work clothes,

---

[3] The expression "knowledge worker" was first introduced by Peter Drucker in
his book "Landmarks of tomorrow." Also refer to Peter Drucker. 1993. *Concept
of the Corporation*, p. xvii.
[4] We will consider it under the heading of IT infrastructure.

containers to the assembly line, and scanners. This equipment can have decisive effects on change. For example, there was a project devoted to increasing employee satisfaction. Some measures were initiated, starting from small gifts to naming the "Employee of the month." None of these measures was able to create the desired improvement in the situation. Our analysis showed that due to increased volumes, the room temperature in the warehouse had plummeted in winter, as the doors were always open. Therefore, it was always uncomfortably cold. Then the management decided to provide employees with newly purchased jackets. This investment immediately resulted in higher employee satisfaction. The effect of equipment is not to be underestimated especially in case of changes propelled by lean management.

Environment

Environment includes the overall, local surroundings in which change has to take place, especially the location of a company or a branch and the cultural environment.

The localization of a workplace can directly affect the planning of a cultural or process change in the company. Thus, process change in the workflow of a manufacturing company had direct influence on the start and end times of shifts. So commuters could not use public transport any more, which in turn had a direct, negative effect on work satisfaction. In this case, organizing a shuttle as an infrastructural measure has promoted commitment of the persons involved and thus ensured that process change could be established.

By cultural environment, we mean country or nationality specifics. How respective nationalities develop with respect to different cultural aspects such as communication, leadership, dealing with time or hierarchies, has been investigated fundamentally by Meyer[5] and Hofsteede.[6] In our context, it is only important to recognize the culture-specific conditions, both of the people concerned as well as of the respective country and to verify their relevance in the respective change.

---

[5]   Erin Meyer. 2015. *The Culture Map*. New York.
[6]   Geert Hofstede et al 2010. *Cultures and Organisations*. New York.

Country specifics particularly play an important role in a multinational environment. The reorganization of office structures with the aim of enabling higher efficiency and faster decisions has led to considerably less resistance in a Scandinavian environment, for example, than in the Asian context.

Another example from the field of continuous improvement tries to clarify the effect of this infrastructural element better: The introduction of team dialogues is based on the assumption that employees point out problems in the dialogue in the sense of continuous improvement and work out solutions together. In a cultural context, which is characterized by lower hierarchy and high individualism as individual responsibility, the effect of cultural country-specifics is low. However, in a culturally hierarchically characterized environment with less individual responsibility, team dialogue finds it difficult to achieve its highest performance in the sense of troubleshooting and finding solutions. Conscious of these cultural barriers, we have taken measures considering cultural dynamics, in the last case. Practically, this means raising problems and problem solutions anonymously and in writing, as cultural prevalence forbids employees from naming a problem in front of the group and in the presence of superiors as this would be perceived as a critique of superiors, which was not intended by the cultural system. However, it was possible to raise problems and to find (real) solutions under anonymity.

The influence of physical infrastructure in the elements of buildings, office, equipment, and environment is supplemented by the IT infrastructure.

IT Infrastructure

In smaller change projects that have no direct effect on IT, there may be no reason to think about the effect of IT infrastructure on change. However, the exponentially increasing relevance of IT suggests that the effect of this infrastructure should be borne in mind in any case. Structurally, hardware, software, and applications must be considered equally here.

The main question that needs to be asked in this context is: What is the way in which (existing) hardware and software enables and supports the change and how must it be adapted to be able to contribute significantly in achieving project goals?

With the help of this printer example, we have already shown how the selection (network printer) and installation (accessible centrally for everybody) of a specific hardware influences change.

Change implications are sometimes significant also in case of software and its applications, especially when change as such includes introduction of a new software. Therefore, for example, major software implementation fails because the program as such contained such major weaknesses that it could not overcome the dysfunctionality. The main question, which every change manager for the respective change should ask, is: Does the respective software or application enable and support the (new) behavior striven for?

In addition to IT infrastructure, process infrastructure is also affected by almost every change or an important influence element.

Process Infrastructure

In reorganization projects, it must first always be clarified as to how the respective department will communicate with one another; how the leadership structures will materialize; or how the respective tasks will be described or be differentiated from one another. In leadership change processes, for example, a new type of decision making is defined in this case. In other change projects, tasks are redistributed or new areas of responsibilities are tailored. There are always specific procedures, routines behind this which have been adapted or should be created, as well as tools that support or constitute the respective processes. The clearer the processes are analyzed and their relevance for change examined and possibly adapted, that much more successful will the project be.

Procedures

Strictly speaking, procedures[7] constitute the respective process. They include both workflows and practices as well as measures and methods. Many

---

[7] In the German edition, I have also used the English term "Procedures," because it contains different aspects, which are not adequately captured by the German words process or procedure.

people do not realize how much our entire life is determined by procedures. One only thinks of the first few minutes of the day: Get up, go to the bathroom, have breakfast, and leave the house—all actions usually follow a clear process structure or a clear procedure. These procedures exist right from the baker to the newspaper deliveryman, for knowledge workers and craftsmen. The first task of change managers, just like the other infrastructure elements, is to identify the existing procedures that enable specific behavior and to analyze their change relevance or their development potential. "Does the existing procedure support change or not?" is guiding question.

We are still at the example of waking up. The change should be that morning routines, from waking up to leaving the house, become stress-free. A first "root cause analysis" shows the following: The actual behavior is characterized by stress that originates from time constraint. This in turn is caused by delayed wake-up, which in turn is the result of sleep deprivation and limited daytime motivation. Within the meaning of MIC methodology, all areas must naturally be worked upon. At this point, we will restrict ourselves to infrastructure and to the procedure in it. The analysis here would specify that both the wake-up time as well as the process of the initial minutes or the breakfast habit need to be changed. The wake-up process, in particular, is adapted by another alarm and different positioning of the same, so that it can only be displayed when the person wakes up. The breakfast process is only adapted in that the preparation is done the evening before and it again saves time. The total saving of time by these measures is 16 minutes. It de-stresses the entire morning routine and change for the long term.

The above example was consciously chosen to show that procedures are multifariously interwoven with our (professional) life, and that their adaption for change can prove to be decisive. As per my observation, existing procedures very often are perceived and analyzed too little. Always when there are recurring processes, which require the same action, make routines from them, which need special attention in change.

Routines

A routine, which is defined by an action or an application becoming a habit by repetition, appears neurobiologically in synapses and nerve paths that have built a Highway. The more often and longer we repeat a specific action, that much stronger the neuronal paths are and that much more effort is required to change them. In this context, the neurobiology of learning is especially interesting, because the change of a routine is mainly nothing other than unlearning the old and learning the new behavior. In the process, the brain finds it principally easier to overwrite old experiences than to give up behavior, without rehearsing a new behavior in its place.

The competence matrix (cf. Figure 4.1) helps in understanding how a new routine is set up. The start of the change journey often lies in determining that one is not aware of lack of competence at all (unconscious incompetence). The new process is still unknown and the inherent inability with regard to this process is also not known, of course. If a new process should now be discovered and then learned, then for the first time one becomes aware that the process is not known as yet (conscious incompetence). This step is decisive and is often felt unpleasant, as one is obliged to leave his or

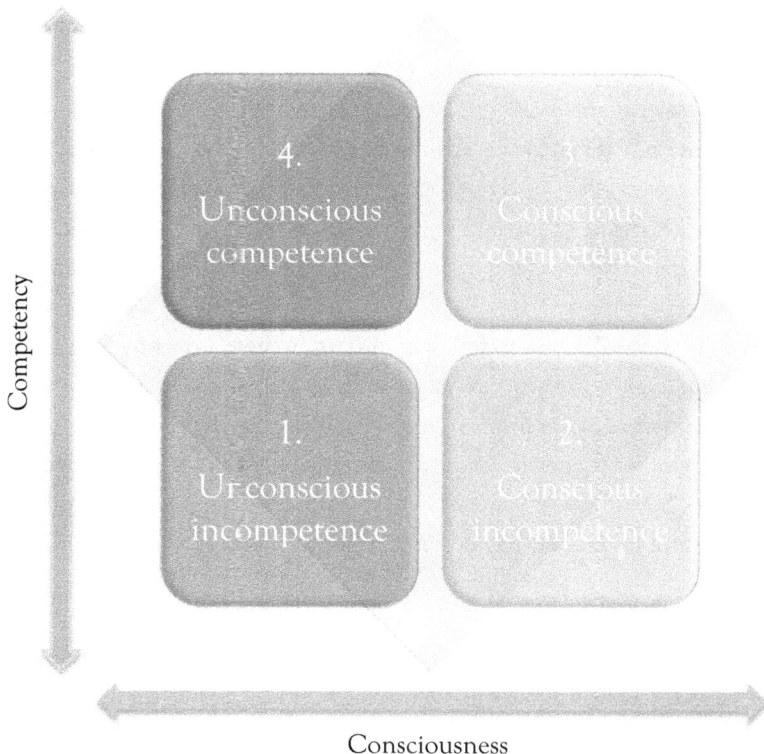

Figure 4.1 *Competence matrix*

her comfort zone. The point now is to get to know the new behavior or in this case the new process and to learn it too. The process of learning must be controlled consciously (conscious competence), as the old behavior is stronger than the new. If the new behavior is rehearsed often enough and over a long enough period, it becomes automatic and becomes a habit (unconscious competence). Therefore, a new routine starts.

Tools

Turning procedures into routines can be supported with the help of suitable tools. A known tool to help routines become a habit is the Standard Operating Procedures (SOP). The procedures describe a specific process, which employees working in this environment have to follow. The challenge with SOP frequently is that though they are written down (somewhere), they are neither really known nor visible or observed in detail. Therefore, they do not create a routine. The reasons are, on the one hand, the lack of understanding of the MIC name, and on the other hand, the description and implementation of the SOP. A person naturally looks for the easier or rehearsed path. As soon as a new path is walked along or another process than the existing one is supposed to be followed, it is associated with effort. It is then accepted if there is a necessity for the new behavior (extrinsic or intrinsic motivation). Here, in addition to the will, the skill is also decisive and a sense of purpose is important for both. If a specific process does not make any sense or if the purpose is not revealed, it then becomes difficult to follow it. It is often the reason why SOP is not followed: Even if the procedures are actually known, they make no sense to the employee or are not practiced sustainably enough.

Every other tool that supports a specific behavior can play a decisive role here. Starting from I-shares, which enable and support team collaboration, through process-related tools[8] right to coaching tools will be dealt with later.[9]

---

[8] In logistics principally and in the warehouse specifically, scanners are, for example, important tools, which support (or hinder) a specific process. Choice, location, and quality of this tool directly affect a process. Digitization has a lot to contribute to process change in the sense of enhancement (e.g., wearables or scan glasses).

[9] Cf. Chapter 5.

Measuring tools play a role not just as part of procedures, rather they are a decisive factor to influence or to change an infrastructure and are therefore dealt with in the next section.

Measurement Infrastructure

The almost banal statement that only the thing which can be measured, can also be improved, proves to be profoundly true and expedient, both in private as well as in professional context. In the business context, Key Performance Indicators (KPIs) and Individual Key Objectives (IKOs) are used for measurement and control of processes. It is somewhat problematic from a change perspective when these infrastructure elements are not supported by mindset and capability elements. Moreover, it comes down to the correct measuring elements that need to be applied correctly and in an integrated manner.

The diet industry is another example from the private sector. Daily measurement of weight is neither sustainable nor expedient, per se. It only works when it is incorporated in other infrastructural elements (such as nutritional monitoring), mindset (such as literature on healthy nutrition), and capability (such as peer-group participation). It therefore follows that the goals and other infrastructural elements integrated in the change need to be especially verified with respect to their substantive coherence with actual change. KPI can be adapted and modified until they have been made "tame" so to say; that is, they are achieved in any case, but do not control change any more.

Objectives

In the formulation of objectives, besides their correctness and relevance, acceptance also needs to be considered.

> ### Case Study
>
> The coaching activity of management should be measured in a project. This infrastructural element is, of course, important from a change perspective. At the same time, it also shows the implementation of all

measurement parameters, the danger of not driving and supporting behavior but degenerating into a formal points-catalog process. The defined objective for every manager in this case was to conduct five coaching dialogues in the week. Whether these took place can be easily measured with the help of an Excel table. As the M and C elements were missing in this case (the concerned person was neither willing nor coached), the number of dialogues conducted did fulfill the specified criteria, but the quality did not meet the expectations. The reason for this was purely extrinsic motivation (monitoring by Excel table). However, to successfully implement this measure, the inner conviction of management with regard to the meaning and purpose of the whole (intrinsic motivation) would have been necessary.

Thus, attitude also affects behavior and vice versa. But can change in behavior and attitude be measured at all? As we have seen already, there are reasoning structures for both actions. Ultimately, only behavioral change can be measured. Mindset-oriented objectives can only be measured indirectly, if at all. For our context, it is important to formulate objectives for change projects not just in a numbers-oriented manner, but also in a behavior-oriented manner. It is illustrated in another example:

Case Study

The executive wanted to encourage more personal initiative in case of a cultural team change. From the classical, hierarchical context, the team was used to waiting for instructions from the executive. This typical "command-and-control" culture always has a clear process structure. Both the executive as well as the employees behave according to the culture: The executive allocates assignments and employees wait for the condition "from above." Demanding more personal initiative—in other words: "I cannot spell everything out—XY should think and decide for themselves"—is not just a new work assignment, but also a culture-altering mindset change—on both sides. The mindset objective could be described here with "Empowerment." Based on this, concrete behavioral objectives were formulated like: "In project X, employee Y goes independently to customer Z and coordinates the project objectives. These are presented to the executive only for his information." Obviously, this objective brought both the executive and the employee out of their comfort zone. The executive wanted to be more involved and the employee would have preferred to have obtained the consent of the executive every now and then. However, since the executive was aware of the individual change dynamics due to intensive coaching, he could alter his behavior and could thus ensure change in his employee's behavior. As explained already, this small behavioral change was part of a cultural change and therefore so challenging. It needed to be ensured that these and similar formulation of objectives were implemented by all employees in several projects over a longer timescale—so the culture could be changed. Formulation of objectives must be complementary in a qualitative as well as a quantitative respect.

The coaching example above has shown that though measurement of the frequency of coaching sessions is important, it needs to be supplemented by qualitative measurements. This could be controlled, for example, by the executive querying his managers, concretely and with regard to content, about positive and challenging coaching experiences. Managers, who only had done a tick-in-the-box drill, felt themselves challenged to dive deep in the contents in the next coaching. At this point, it needs to be noted once again that influencing strategies support the freedom of the person at the most. Those who do not *want* to change their attitude cannot and should not be forced to do so.

Formulation of objectives is also important as part of infrastructure, but it comes down to the manner of formulation, its alignment to behavior, and verifiability. Part of formulation of objectives in change is performance measurement.

Performance Management

Usually, objectives of projects as well as strategic programs are measured and controlled by KPI. There are diverse concepts and views with regard to the effectiveness of such control elements. An empirical approach is followed at this point without discussing the theoretical background. A simple measurement of performance change already induces, as per our experience. At best, it becomes clear in the so-called performance dialogues. If they were able to enable widespread acceptance for the concept, they were a helpful support in controlling behavior. Even the weight reduction programs mentioned earlier have measurement (weighing) of performance as an important element. In leadership programs as well, we have always determined that data-fed measurements as such already lead to initial changes by measurement. If additional objectives (KPIs) are then formulated, activities then always lead to real changes in behavior, if the objectives are shared and accepted by all. The "What's-in-it-for-me" especially must not just be discussed but must be developed in such a way that it is emotionally ingrained in the concerned persons.

Rewarding and Recognition Infrastructure

In the section "Motivating Leadership" (Chapter 3) we have already spoken about intrinsic and extrinsic motivation or shown with the help of Pinks studies why the effect of financial incentive systems is limited and why "Autonomy, Mastery, and Purpose" motivate more deeply and sustainably.

Principally, for a positive result or behavior achieved, the rewarding and recognition infrastructure always aims to give the employee a reward that acknowledges the person or performance, which in turn is supposed to reciprocally influence his motivation or the motivation of his colleagues. The different forms of this appreciation can be divided into four elements: reward, recognition, bonus, and awards.

The German word *Belohnung* (reward) has the noun "lohn," which indicates remuneration. Financial remuneration, however, does not automatically mean a reward. In further psychological sense, the system of reward/punishment can be referenced. Classical conditioning happens by rewarding good or desired behavior and punishing the bad or undesired behavior. The effectiveness of scorecards and other reward systems in the private consumer sector is known and their behavior-guiding and modifying effect is proven sufficiently. This mechanism is repeated oft and successfully in the economic or corporate context. The following examples can be mentioned based on our observations:

- Employees or teams can earn points by specific performance or specific behavior, which bring a gift.
- Special performance is rewarded by shopping vouchers or electronic appliances.
- A short vacation was also a part of the incentive system.
- After successful completion of training or a project, employees get a certificate signed by the CEO.

Sometimes, employees are singled out for special performance and chosen as "Employee of the month." These and similar **rewards** can have an ambivalent effect. For one, it is not appropriate for employees to be singled out from their colleagues and to be publicly "honored." On the other hand, the criteria that have led to this choice are not always recognized by all and may even have the opposite effect ("He was not that good ..."). In a feedback culture marked by honesty, in which one can be happy about a special performance of a colleague instead of being envious, this infrastructural tool in contrast can be very behavior controlling.

Recognition is rather the personalized expression of gratitude for specific behavior or a service rendered. Being recognized also means being accepted and respected or esteemed. Recognition also corresponds to deep human yearning, in the sense of deeper perception of being "seen." Even the facial expression of a superior can bestow this recognition to an employee—without a physical gift being presented or even a word being spoken.

An interesting form of recognition is the so-called fuck-up-night originating in the context of start-ups and innovation. Normally, success and performance are recognized. But here, failure and defeat are recognized. The effect of this infrastructural element on change is clear once more. In the German context especially, sometime a misunderstanding can be observed here: Mistakes in orientation are not rewarded and acclaimed, that they are best repeated immediately as per the old logic. In fact, rewarding creative and innovative energy of enterprise and courage are in focus—which unfortunately have led to failure/defeat. Precisely since failure is celebrated, the sharp sting is taken out of failure for participants and so perceptibly that the risk of trying and the courage for innovation enable something else—and therefore failure is not so dramatic or, in this sense, can even be interpreted positively as a learning experience.

Bonus in the corporate context is rather a ritualistic or institutionalized form of rewarding performance. There are also forms where performance is also included at least in the bonus. Here, however, the question arises from known reasons (cf. Pinks examinations, section "Motivating Leadership" in Chapter 3), whether behavior-related bonus does not have a rather counterproductive effect. For example, a bonus could be linked to exemplary leadership behavior, which is defined by consistent past practice of certain behaviors such as commitment, target orientation, and so on. The question is how this behavior can be measured consistently. Even a feedback system, which could most likely lead to an objective result, if it contains the feedback of several persons, is unreliable, because the employee is well aware that his feedback will determine the material bonus by superiors. Still, bonus, at least in the context of bigger enterprises, is an important control element from a socioeconomic perspective: All employees know and sense that they are joint contributors to the company's success—there at least bonus can contribute toward desired behavior.

Special awards are often important events for employees. If they are communicated accordingly and are recognized in the organization, they contribute to behavioral change in the change. As in the case of all reward mechanisms, the question also arises here: Does the award actually effect a fundamental change in attitude or does it lead superficially to a desired result, but is not sustainable? As always, it comes down to context. As soon as the reward elements are linked with other mindset and capability elements, the probability of a deeper transformation in behavior increases dramatically because the people affected by change experience authenticity and congruence of the target state.

Organizational Design Infrastructure

Training and recruitment are described once again in greater detail in Chapter 5.[10] Here, the roles of employees and other elements of the organizational structure should be dealt with.

Personnel and Team Structure

It is not just in team changes, but also usually in all other major change measures that new role descriptions are necessary. For one, it is naturally important to determine the roles and to describe them with regard to their peculiar characteristic as well as their relationship with other roles and to set this down in writing. It is at least as much important to discuss these roles (descriptions) with the respective employees as to get their input. Thereby, this tool can actually support a real behavioral change. A discussion on roles will include employees in the process and obtain or integrate their feedback. If employees have more creative options in planning and execution, it will lead to greater identification with the change.

The team structure is determined together with the roles. This includes the reporting structure, cooperation, (self) organization, and communication.

In less hierarchically structured companies and particularly start-ups, the thematization of the reporting structure alone may sound unrealistic. Self-organized teams, holacracy structures, or scrum teams need no or few reporting structures. However, they are widespread in classic companies and especially in large corporations. Organizational changes, restructuring, and cultural change programs particularly also affect the

---

[10] As infrastructural element, it needs to be said here that how people are trained for change and to what extent this training becomes part of their routine needs to be given importance, particularly in major change processes. It is again stressed that it is essential to provide the right employees with the right talents at the right time and who are correctly trained for the change. Personnel provision and development measures are often incorrectly connected with change; rather, they are simultaneously controlled by the personnel department. However, it is more effective to make personnel development part of change and to liberate them from the usual processes for the duration of change.

responsibility and hierarchy levels. In change programs, which bring about more personal initiative by employees and overcome silo mentality, classic reporting structures are replaced by agile team forms, where teams are formed from different function, with functional leadership. In any case, analysis and review of reporting structures are important with respect to their effects on change in every change, and particularly in both directions: to what extent is the existing reporting structure influenced by the change or the existing structure or the structure to be changed influences the change.

How do teams collaborate? Usually, there are—consciously or unconsciously—processes: organizational and relationship structures. The process structures decide the path that work will follow. For example, employee A edits a document and forwards it to B. Or employees C and D create a new product wherein they work alternately individually and jointly for the creation. Organization structures affect team meetings, "offsites" and office environment (which has already been dealt with in detail elsewhere; see the section "Routines"). Relationship structures affect the real, true relational level. Members of the same team must not be friends. Nevertheless, it can be immediately perceived whether the team is forced to collaborate or whether trust, appreciation, and acceptance prevail. Process and organization structures in particular are examined in change projects for their relevance to the success of the project. If the processes and the team organization do not support the change, then they must be adapted. Communication is also part of the relationship organization: How, when, and what is communicated—all team members should be aware of that and must live that.

Self-organized teams are in vogue as part of agile structures. This has been referred to here because this is a separate and major topic, and good literature has been available[11] meanwhile.

Policies are especially important for larger companies, safety-relevant environments, or complex tasks. The larger a system is, the more frameworks are specified—and so let chaos have space. The more safety has a

---

[11] Siegfried Kaltenecker. 2018. *Leading Self-Organised Teams*. Heidelberg. Kaltenecker. 2017. *Self-Organised Company*. Heidelberg. Astrid Vermeer. 2017. *Self-Organised Teams in Practice*. Den Haag.

role, that much clearer must processes, organization, and human behavior be coordinated and must complement each other, so that they provide a consistent result. Increasing complexity needs policies to also avoid chaotic, unwanted incidents, and results. The more important such policies are, their direct influence on change is sometimes overestimated. Our observation tells us that they are particularly important to safeguard the sustainability of change. Similarly, there are certain types of personality, whose rules and clear job descriptions offer security and thereby reduce resistance to change.

Summary

In every change, it is important to examine and adapt the infrastructure in addition to the mindset.

Three steps summarize the most important elements:

1. Discover enabling/hindering infrastructures
   - According to the above-mentioned elements, it is about identifying the infrastructure elements that support the new behavior.
   - It is also important to identify the elements that hinder the desired behavior.

2. Eliminate the hindering elements or at least reduce their effect
   - The infrastructure elements that do not support the change must be changed, adapted, or eliminated.
   - Non-supportive elements are replaced by supportive elements.

3. The enabling elements strengthen and support
   - Existing infrastructure elements that support change are strengthened.
   - If necessary, *new* infrastructures are established which support the change success.

CHAPTER 5

Capability

To be able to cope with change, the concerned people do not just need the right mindset and supporting infrastructure, but also the will, skill or proficiency, flair, talent, capability, and the ability. All these terms reflect the characteristics of capability. Apart from the word ability, wherein an element of training of a skill not present before also resonates, with the other terms one gets the impression that they describe something that is naturally present—or possibly not. Talented people do not learn, but they have an "innate' ability, which others do not have—which is the conventional wisdom. Recent research has shown that this view does not correspond with the present state of scientific understanding.[1] Emotional intelligence or mindfulness itself, which could be retained as a characteristic or at least an innate quality, can be learned, as mentioned already.[2]

This is why the question for every change is: What must the concerned employees be able to do and what helps them to learn it—if they are not able to do it? This capability must also be understood in a broader sense: What must an organization be able to do to be ready for the future? The "capability" of an organization thus extends mainly to the infrastructure and the persons. We have already dealt with the "capability" of the infrastructure. Here, we mainly want to focus on the "capability" of the employees. As management support is central in case of every change, it is first about leadership skills.[3] Then, we differentiate between knowledge and capability, as both elements are important in the change project, but may be frequently separated. As feedback and coaching are central in

---

[1] Cf. Werner Siefer: Das Talent in mir. Warum Talent erlernbar ist. Frankfurt 2009.

[2] Chade-Meng Tan. 2014. *Search Inside Yourself.* New York.

[3] Skills include abilities, talents, and especially professional expertise such as negotiation skill.

every change, these tools must be explained separately, should be mentioned again specifically just like the topic of "Learning," as it represents a major change motivator.

Leadership Skills

The ability to connect with People

One needs specific abilities for specific change. At this point now, it is not about special leadership skills, which are only necessary for specific change—for example, basic knowledge with respect to digitalization in digital transformation—rather it is about fundamental management abilities, which are relevant in every change. What management is and how one best describes the qualities that a manager should have, can be read in Fredmund Malik.[4] In the process, it is less about talent for leadership, which is important for changes. Especially, the aspects of emotional intelligence and attentiveness are only peripheral. The attitudes and activities described by Malik, which lead to effective management, may fit for a particular managerial style and for a particular type of personality; however, the leadership qualities necessary for change movements refer to another human level and go beyond pure numbers and result-oriented management. Not that these aspects would be unimportant, since even in change, achieving results is essential. Leadership qualifications, which moreover mean that people are taken along on the journey of change and get involved, are named too little in many—even good—management concepts, from our perspective. Malik refers to management in general, not to CM in particular.

Before we delve deeper into the concepts of emotional intelligence and attentiveness, we would like to demonstrate seven behavioral patterns, which we repeatedly observed in practice in those executives who have best managed changes and executed them successfully. These behavioral patterns do not contradict the fundamentals of effective leadership

---

[4]   Fredmund Malik best summarizes the topic of effective management: *Managing Performing Living.* Campus 2015.

such as result orientation, holistic thinking, focusing, strength orientation, trust or positive thinking; but they take them for granted and go beyond that.

> *Principally, it is about one great ability, which emotionally intelligent, sensitive and extremely successful executives always demonstrate: The ability to connect with people and to remain connected to them.*

At first, this observation may surprise or even be rejected, as leadership is classically connected with hierarchy, counterpart, command and criticism, warning and challenge. The language also shows us: If we can start something with a term, if it appears that we have an image of it, or if related terms and descriptions occur to us, we connect something with the term. Similarly, we connect a feeling or an impression with a person. From neurobiology, we know that when there is consensus between two people, the neurons of one reflect in the other.[5] By "To be able to connect with a person," we mean in our context precisely this empathetic emotional ability of being able to deal with a wide variety of persons with different attitudes and characteristics, understanding them from inside out, to be able to give them this feeling of being understood, communicating at eye level[6] and to thus be able to influence the mindset of these persons. This skill in the sense of proficiency and ability includes listening and understanding, also includes the ability of being able to adapt individual style of leadership to a specific person and situation, of being able to be a role model, having the desire and ability of being able to develop others, being able to give them direction and the skill and the will to learn and try.

---

[5] See, for example, Christian Keysers. 2011. *The Empathic Brain. How the Discovery of Mirror Neurons Changes Our Understanding of Human Nature.* Lexington

[6] This means that each dialogue partner feels accepted as a person and not just in his role.

Listening

In addition to the Four Ears model of Friedemann Schulz-von-Thun[7] (2010), which generally describes the sender–receiver problem, there is a myriad of models that thematize different types of listening. We would like to explain two prominent models at this point:

Otto Scharmer's Four-Level Model[8]:

1. **Download**: At this level, listening is such that own assumptions are confirmed.
2. **Factual**: Objective listening turns toward the new, and is open for distinction.
3. **Empathic**: Empathic listening enables seeing a thing or a person from the perspective of another. Attention passes from listener to speaker and enables a deep connection at different levels.
4. **Generative**: This deep level of listening goes far beyond "listening." It is used as a synergy, essence, or flow between two or more dialogue partners.

Stephen Covey[9] differenties Five Levels of Listening:

- **Level 1—Ignoring:** There is no listening, just waiting, when one can say something again. One is busy with one's own thoughts while the dialogue partner is talking.
- **Level 2—Pretending:** One nods to give the appearance that he is listening, but is actually self-absorbed.

---

7   Friedemann Schulz von Thun: Miteinander reden: Störungen und Klärungen. Psychologie der zwischenmenschlichen Kommunikation. Rowohlt, Reinbek 1981.
8   C. Otto Scharmer. 2018. *The Essentials of Theory U: Core Principles and Applications*. Oakland.
9   Stephen Covey. 1989/2004. *7 Habits of Highly Effective People*. New York.

- **Level 3—Selective Listening**: Only individual topics are paid more attention; as soon as interest in that reduces, one returns to level 1 or 2.
- **Level 4—Attentive Listening**: One really listens to the speaker, concentrates on what he is saying.
- **Level 5—Empathic Listening**: Not just the words uttered, but the emotions behind them are also perceived. There is more listening than speaking.

It is not the intention of this book to question this (or even other) models as regards their coherence or everyday suitability. At this point, it is only about showing that there are different levels of listening and that normal everyday conversation, which includes management conversation, often moves on the initial levels. However, the capability required for change lies on a deeper level in any case.

Being able to connect with people starts with the means of communication deemed by most as the main medium, language. In the corporate context, communication is sometimes mainly perceived from the "Sender" perspective. As suggested by the models shown, the receiver's perspective is also important, especially when it is about empathic listening. True to the motto: "How should I know what I think, before I hear what I say?"[10] A deep connection forms and grows between people, the more they learn to listen. This listening can now adopt different dimensions in everyday life. The more a manager has learnt to listen with focus and at a deeper level, the better this will qualify him in managing major changes. The objective here is to arrive at the level of attentive, generative, or empathic listening. As part of the chapter on emotional intelligence and attentiveness, we will also speak about the fact that these characteristics can be learned and taught. According to our experience, this first characteristic, in particular, that of being able to connect with people, is central to managing changes in the best possible manner and to making them successful. One of the main observations with respect to the question of how far successful and less successful change projects differ from

---

[10]   That is the title of the extremely interesting book by Franca Parianen.

one another always concerns the quality of leadership. Moreover, this has little to do with actual qualification; it rather involves the seven elements of good change leadership. However, the more prominent one here is the ability to listen. The capability of listening ensures one of the most important preconditions necessary for change: Trust. Real listening gives root to another quality, which is significant for being able to connect with people: Understanding people deeply.

Understanding—Be Able to "Read People"

Generative listening described by Otto Scharmer makes it clear as to how real listening is a purely passive act on the receiver side. If there is a flow between two people, synergy becomes perceivable and the sender–receiver perspective is expanded to a deeper third level—understanding. A new dynamic is then effective, which results from the ability of being able to "Read people."[11] According to Albert Mehrabian, interpersonal communication includes 7 percent content, 38 percent voice, and 55 percent body language with respect to effect.[12] The ability of being able to "read" people and decipher them makes up 93 percent of communication. Many executives may be cognitively aware of this relationship of communicative perception or it may at least appear logical to them. The art is solely in the application. Communication is too often on a purely content-related level in management processes, fundamentally and in change processes particularly. Sometimes, it is unconsciously perceived that not everything is correctly understood; however, there is a powerlessness or even an inability to respond holistically to people (or groups) in communication. Practicing deeper understanding of people starts with training the awareness of 93 percent of communication comprising voice and body language. Perceiving is followed by showing understanding.

---

[11] "Reading people" in this context means to be able to perceive people holistically, mainly with respect to their body language, and to be able to understand them deeply.

[12] Mehrabian, A. 1967. "Susan Ferris: Inference of Attitude from Nonverbal Communication in Two Channels." *The Journal of Counselling Psychology* 31, no. 3, pp. 248–52.

The impression of being understood in turn deepens the level of communication and creates a still deeper understanding. The ability of being able to read people also includes correctly reflecting or applying that what is "read." Understanding is performative communication par excellence!

The important thing is to emphasize that understanding is conveyed in the rarest of cases by verbalizing it ("I understand you"). As understanding originates from emotional proximity, regard, respect, and the will to understand or the ability to engage with the opposite person, cognitive lingual expression can sum up the event and intensify present understanding, but cannot produce it linguistically. Those who do not feel understood will understand every linguistic assurance ("I understand you") in the exactly opposite manner.

Understanding a person or even a situation deeply requires another, additional leadership quality: that of engaging differently with different persons and situations and being able to adapt a style of leadership accordingly.

Person and Situation—Appropriate Leadership Style

The ability of forging a deep connection with people is challenged first by the diversity of people and their characteristic traits. Personality models like Discovery Insights, DISC, Enneagramm, Reiss-Profile, Humm-Wadsworth personality model, MBTI, The Big Five, and many more show from different angles how diverse people are with respect to diverse characteristic traits such as extroversion or diligence, attention to detail or emotionalism, or how differently they respond to people or situations. The multitude of models with all sorts of typologies shows that there is a constant attempt to squeeze persons and their characteristics in diagrams and matrices, whereby none of the models will be able to illustrate all the personality traits. Thus, the recognition of limits of the model rather speaks for the integrity of the same. From a leadership perspective, it is definitely useful to master at least one or two models and not to just have heard of them in a 2-day seminar. A personality model can provide initial assistance such as a coordinate system to (better) understand a person. At the same time, certainty of the relativity of each model is fundamental, because perception, for one, may be wrong and, on the other hand, every person is different from what is dictated by the typology of a personality model. Therefore, the meta perspective of attitude and behavior appropriate for the person is more important: Regardless of (maybe obvious from a particular personality model) type profile, the executive tries to speak the "language" of the person, that is, he tries to integrate the attitudes, opinions, and characteristic features, on which personality is based, into the communication. From neurolinguistic programming (NLP), one knows that similar communication models that take into account the unique personality of the opposite person create a harmony at a subconscious level, which at a conscious level enables a person to feel understood by his communication partner, thereby establishing an interpersonal connection.

This is elucidated with an example of a typology of the DISC model. The I-type is the "big-picture" person; a creative personality who wants to look far into the future and diversely too, but who is deterred by high levels of detail such as critical attitudes ("Nothing is impossible"). Regardless of individual type, communication must be about speaking exactly this "language." "Language," not just in the linguistic sense but also in the holistic sense, encompasses feelings, ideas, and attitudes. Convincing an "I" person for a change or influencing him in this direction will be less successful if the risks are outlined and the minute details of change are demonstrated. An "I" personality is rather convinced by the broader vision and a "Yes, we can do that" attitude. A conscientiousness person is convinced in a completely different manner for the same change. The conscientiousness will be about every minute detail and one can ask him specifically what risks he anticipates for the success of the project.

This example of a DISC type is supposed to illustrate that empathic recognition by the executive of the personality type to be attributed to the opposite person, and corresponding choice of the typological address, creates a basis to forge a connection with the person.

In other words: The better one knows what makes the opposite person "tick" and the better one is able to speak the "language" of the opposite person, that much faster and deeper is a connecting and trustworthy relation established, which on its part again is a precondition to increase acceptance by the opposite person for change—and that is the ultimate objective of leadership in change: to support people through the emotional curve of change in such a way that more people and concerned persons go through change more effectively, thus resulting in higher acceptance.

At this point, one could interject that this type of leadership is manipulative and utilitarian. The answer is: Each type of leadership is manipulative in the sense of being influencing. It can be considered manipulative in the morally negative and unjustifiable sense if it does not respect the freedom of people or leads toward morally unacceptable goals. Leadership is utilitarian insofar as it is not the job of leadership to make employees happy; leadership is not there for the sake of it, but it follows a clear objective in the economic context: to lead effectively to increase market share, to improve productivity, and to become more economically viable. Leadership in the context of change supports this objective; however, it also tries to take people along on this journey.

Good leadership is not just capable of engaging with various personalities, but also with a multitude of different situations, so that it can again establish a better connection with people through this process.

Here, it is not any situation related to the operational workday, but people undergoing change. In change processes, there are three main paradigmatic situations that an executive has to deal with: The situation descriptions correspond to phases of the emotional change curve, whereby it is not about detailed ascription to the respective phase in this connection, but about the rough description of the main reactions to change. Moreover, we distinguish the reaction into individual, directed toward individuals or small groups, and group reaction. The threshold is marked by the stakeholder: If individuals show the same change reaction or are present in the same phase, then the individual reaction is correct; in heterogeneous units, it is the group reaction.

How Does Leadership Appear Along the Change Curve?

The first change situation is described by "denying." This is the typical initial reaction to change. Change is not recognized or taken seriously; it is denied actively or passively. As executives often initiate change or are held responsible for it at least, they are automatically considered to be the "other side"; it creates distance and makes connecting difficult.

In individual meetings, it is important at this point to demonstrate the seriousness of change. Employees have experienced too often that changes are not really desired or cease relatively quickly. When leadership is convinced of seriousness, veracity, and probability of success of the change, they are supposed to make it visible and clear in individual meetings. Here, employees will pay attention to the consistency and congruence of the message. Verbal or nonverbal delegation of responsibility ("The Board has decided," "That's just the way it is," etc.) does not help, for one, to get consent for the change and on the other hand does not support the efforts to build a real connection.

Straightforward information is important when the executive meets groups who are in the "denying" situation (generally speaking). What exactly is the change all about, what will change and what will remain the same, what is known and what is not—these are questions, honest answers of which are conducive to correct information.

If individuals or groups are a situation of "resistance," then it is an unpleasant situation for the persons concerned. They feel that they need to change, but do not want to or do not know where this journey will lead them or how they will "seem" as a person in the future. It is important in personal meetings to relate to the emotional situation of the employee. Genuine empathy always involves professional distance, without lapsing into a negative sentimental spiral. "Understanding" from the previous section once again gets emotional depth here. Showing understanding springs from an emotional concern, which does not propose hasty solutions to evade the unpleasant feeling. In groups especially, it can be helpful to name the pain points (why the team must be dissolved, old systems replaced, spatial and content-related changes driven, personal habits abandoned).

As the situation of "discovering" is directly connected to this phase and its declared objective is to bring as many employees as quickly as possible and as effectively as possible to this phase, elements of this phase are also present in the previous one. Although the boundaries are fluid, there are main orientations in the respective change situation. In "resistance" it is rather about showing personal concern and identifying emotions, whereas in "discovering" it is about demonstrating how persons can contribute to change or can develop themselves further.

Table 5.1 Leading along the change curve

Change situation	Individual	Group
Gainsay	Serious challenge	Genuine information
Resist	Personal concern	Emotional naming
Discover	Potential contribution	Development opportunities

When individuals open themselves up to change and carefully start asking questions as to how they can participate in the change, the executive will recommend these precise options to them of contributing or help them to discover these options. However, before we start talking about training needs for example, we have to first deal with small opportunities to get to know the future change situation and to understand how a person can contribute with his individual abilities. Development opportunities can be demonstrated in groups, which show the concerned persons that they can retrieve their position in the future by means of further self-development.

The change situations have been deliberately shown in a simplified manner, as it is not about precise instructions by leadership in this context, but about the basic ability to engage with, both a great variety of persons as well as most varied change situations and to be able to respond accordingly (Table 5.1).

Being a Role Model (Role-Modeling)

According to our observation, those executives, who are perceived as a role model in the change, are also those who can establish a connection. The English word "role-modeling" points to an important aspect: It is all about developing yourself in a (role model) role. The decisive factor in change projects is whether the executives are successful in standing up for and standing behind the change. The coherence between word and deed is especially very critical to success here. Our observation tells us that many executives are well aware of their role as a role model. What a person has not experienced himself, he cannot expect from his employees. There is yet another important nuance to the role model role in change processes. Changes are implemented often in a top-down manner in corporations and often as one of many priorities. The challenge lies in making a change program a continuous priority, not letting it abate and letting it appear in minor communications and everyday behavior. Ultimately, it is only possible if the executive does not have to motivate himself for the change, because he is deeply convinced of it and lives this conviction naturally.

Case Study

A cultural engagement program was implemented in different ways in different business divisions of a company. In division A, though there was formal support of the top executives, the employees increasingly felt that the program had no special priority. In division B, it was observed from the beginning that the program was supported and lived through all hierarchies by all the executives. This could be seen in small details such as continuous commendable mention of the program up to reward ceremonies, which were attended by many Board members even after many years.

Real "role-modeling" is based on authentic leadership. This creates trust, which in turn is the basis for real relationships. In real relationships, people can bond with one another, which on its part ensures that people accept change in a better and faster manner.

Being Able and Willing to Develop Others

A big help for people on the change voyage is discovering the opportunity of enhancing oneself. Not every change brings positive change opportunities for every employee. On the contrary, it may sometimes happen that in a changed working situation, full potential could not be displayed or the new work environment does not match the extent of the employee's capabilities as it usually does. At this point, it is the attitude of the executive that is important first, to *want* to enhance the employee fundamentally. It will, which must naturally materialize in due course, show respect on the one hand, and desire on the other hand, to benefit the employee. This attitude again requires trust.

Being *able* to enhance employees first requires looking into what they need and possessing the means for implementation, and second it includes a structural precondition such as job-specific preconditions or organization specifics such as a job change or further training.

As part of change projects, it is not important to approve further education for every employee, but rather to keep an eye on and to ensure the enhancement of employees.

Show Direction — Be a Visionary

Leadership is mainly expected to show direction or create and share a vision for the future. Naturally, it also goes for change projects. The ability to design the future in such a way that it enthuses the employees and helps them imagine the new future during the present change can and should be developed among executives. Too often, the future of change is demonstrated in abstract numbers, too few change stories are narrated, which on their part address people a lot more and help in positively designing personal change. Naturally, the authenticity of the visionary is again decisive. If the executive himself is not convinced of the future, he cannot provide any direction or rather, the development and demonstration of the vision will not reflect in the relationship with the employees.

Wanting to and Being Able to Learn and Try

Executives, who have the ability or who have learnt to establish a relationship with people, eventually create and promote an atmosphere of learning and trying. Being able to try out the freedom of not having to delve into discussions and projects with complete, error-free concepts presupposes the courage of making mistakes. Here, it is not about making mistakes deliberately and being happy about the mistakes as such, but about the courage of treading new paths, not overlooking all the important elements in the process and looking toward creating something new, and not toward mistakes happening. Executives who "live" this spirit exude that perfectionism is not above the person. Making mistakes relieves pressure and again supports a connection of trust that on its part motivates to top performance.

The topic of continuous improvement attaches very little importance to this human dynamic. Pleas of wanting or needing to get better fizzle out, as they are atmospherically not covered for the reasons mentioned. When employees come to know that they can learn and make mistakes, another kind of motivation comes into being, that of making things better.

Emotional Intelligence

Daniel Goleman is considered *the* reference writer[13] on the topic of emotional intelligence, which can be learned, according to his research. Here, he distinguishes five different levels: self-awareness, emotion management, self-motivation, empathy, and relationship management. *Self-awareness* is all about getting to know and becoming aware of your own world of feelings; *emotion management* aims at regulating and influencing your own emotions; *self-motivation* deals with the fact that your own emotions can be used for the service of achieving a goal; *empathy* is the ability of being able to perceive other people's emotions; and the resulting *relationship management* can "manage" emotions of others.

The following main points are central in our context:

- For change, decisive leadership qualities such as being able to listen, being able to perceive body-language signals, or being able to influence people positively can be learned.
- Each strategy for empathy and influence presupposes a high degree of. A person who does not know himself cannot discern others; a person who cannot perceive himself cannot perceive others; a person who cannot manage himself cannot manage others.
- Every case of management of emotions, be they your own or others' emotions, is preceded by the perceptiveness of the same. It is important to the extent the desire for change remains and, as often happens in management, quick results have to be achieved. However, self-awareness and external perception require time. Plants do not grow faster if you pull

---

[13]   Goleman, D. 1996. "Emotional Intelligence." *Why It Can Matter More than IQ.* London.

them out of the ground every day to check their growth or
if you pull them up to hasten their growth. The same laws of
nature govern spiritual and personal growth.

Emotionally intelligent executives are a big contributing factor in the
success of every change. *How* a change is led and managed matters in the
employees' acceptance for change. Executives who understand that they
have to govern themselves and are capable of understanding other people
deeply are accepted and respected. This respect in turn brings about the
trust that employees have to show for leadership in the change processes.
Therefore, it makes sense to invest in relevant trainings for executives.
These investments pay off several times in the long term.

Mindfulness

Recently since Google has prominently thematized the topic of mindfulness,[14] there is a great and increasing demand by corporations and
other organizations for this soft topic. As regards content, it is closely
related to the topic of emotional intelligence, but is first inward looking:
First, it is about training mindfulness through meditation. The meditation taught here does not follow any spiritual school of thought, but
it is about simple awareness and becoming aware of the moment, the
body, and situations. The exercises propounded by Chade-Meng Tan[15]
are, so to say, a direct way with specific exercises to learn emotional
intelligence. First, it is not about making employees happy (even if it is
the consequence). It is more about optimizing life, which then is also
reflected in the profession. People who practice mindfulness work in a
more focused manner, and their communication is more effective, are
more resilient, more resistant to stress, and more motivated. According
to a (verbal) statement by SAP, who has implemented mindfulness with
a lot of success, the return on investment (ROI) is in the range of many
multimillions.

---

[14] For this, refer to Chade-Meng Tan. 2014. *Search Inside Yourself.* New York.
[15] Ibid.

The 3E model

Since self-awareness is a precondition for external perception and as leadership presupposes self-management, I have prepared a model that has already helped frequently in a variety of change projects to generate change in the leadership team. It has often been observed that though executives do lead the change at best, they still have many reservations in their mind and are not at all convinced themselves. The 3E model demonstrates that every change starts with oneself and here especially with the executive. When the executive himself has become aware of his own resistances and has overcome them in the best case, only then can he empathize with others, understand their resistances to overcome them.

- **Embrace**: The attitudes of the executives are examined by means of a self-assessment regarding what is their stand toward the change, what reservations they have, how much they believe in the change, or what they would like to modify.
- **Empathize**: This dimension helps executives imagine themselves in the employee's position to understand his reservations and how they can be overcome.
- **Engage**: In recognizing your own concerns and the resistance of the people concerned, strategies are sought to find solutions that create a win–win situation for all parties involved and which help the change in becoming a reality.

The Knowledge

What employees affected by change can and must know is the main question that we want to deal with under the larger keyword "capability." We have already seen that leadership qualities are mainly needed. When employees affected by change are aware of the necessity of change and want to change themselves with respect to the new behavior, they must know and understand what is new about the change and learn to apply it.

Here is an example from a private environment to start with: Alex's wife Andrea has requested him to be more proactive in his social relationships. Although Alex had a lot of resistance against this request by his wife, it has done a lot of good so far from the change perspective. First, it could create an awareness that better relations with friends and acquaintances would be very beneficial to their own relationship and to their well-being, so that finally Alex is willing and ready to invest more in relationships. The willingness is already present. However, Alex wonders how to go about it and what it exactly means to be more proactive and to invest in relationships. Andrea organizes a course: "Living in relationships—how introverts learn to come out of their shells." In this course, Alex initially understands how relationships form, the basics of communication, and in one course element, he even learns the basics of small talk. This is the knowledge that Alex did not have until now and which he could build on in a specific training. Naturally, it does not mean that he is a social animal now, who *can* always apply the new knowledge acquired. More on this will be discussed later.

Even in the context of the company, knowledge building is usually achieved by training. However, we do not want to regard knowledge building as such; we rather want to pursue the question how capabilities, which are necessary for a specific change, are shaped. In the change context, therefore, the leading question is: What must people affected by change do better or differently and how do they learn that? Here, knowledge and capability go hand in hand. The "new" that is learned by persons affected by change can be a new system, a new method, a new manner of working, a new process, or a new behavior. The necessity of learning something new and acquiring it is common to all change situations. Before a new behavioral pattern is rehearsed and "acquired," it must be known, that is, this knowledge must first be built on.

Knowledge Building

Knowledge building does not happen just by training; rather, it can also be achieved by means of other formats such as reading, web-based learning, learning-by-doing, discussions, or other workshop formats.

Knowledge Building by Training

The usual training situation comprises a trainer who possesses specific knowledge/skills methods and participants who are instructed in this topic precisely. Training also particularly includes the dimension of rehearsing. From the change perspective, in particular, it cannot be expected that new competencies be imbued within a day or a week in such a way that they can be subsequently integrated in the personality and can be applied perfectly.

Case Study

Different business divisions from different countries are merged in a cultural change. Earlier, there used to be *one* country's dominance and thus *one* language. The addition of other business divisions from other countries results in the necessity of consistently introducing English as a common language basis. One of the resistances lies in the limited language competency of many members of the original organization. Now, language courses do not just impart knowledge about the language and a competence in understanding, but also want the language to be rehearsed (capability).

We have frequently observed two conflicting trends in change: the over and under estimation of training. Sometimes, CM is equated with communication or even training. A lot is expected from training in case of IT-intensive changes in particular. Our experience tells us that trainings are only especially successful when the necessary fundamental communication was worked on before: What is the change, why do we need it, how is it implemented, what are the leading questions? If too little attention is paid to the change dynamics, then the training room will hold employees, who either are completely unaware about the change or their resistance level is so high that training makes no sense because either they learn too little or nothing at all. The other trend is that of underestimating training: New behavior is expected from employees, without supporting them in learning; or, it is assumed that they will teach themselves the new behavior.

An example from everyday leadership: "coaching" as the new buzzword is expected explicitly or implicitly by management. However, on the one hand, its precise meaning is not clear, and on the other hand, it is pretended as if "Leading by Coaching" is an intrinsic ability to be produced by the all-round competent manager. Scant notice is taken of the fact that the so-called soft skills such as coaching, listening, balancing, mindfulness, value-based leading, and so on are abilities that require comprehensive training and practicing, just like learning a language. Moreover, even if a manager takes part in a two-day training on the topic of coaching, it does not automatically mean that he already has the requisite coaching competence. It can only be developed by application and practice.

Training is required in most of the change projects to the correct extent and at the correct point, as almost every change asks for new behavior, which has to be acquired. However, training in changes is only effective when it is integrated overall in the MIC change architecture and when it includes a preparatory and a follow-up phase:

- **Training preparation:** As regards communication, the why question needs to be answered here. The content of training is agreed upon with the participants and it mainly needs to be checked whether and to what extent is the topic relevant for the participants.
- **Training execution:** "Test–teach–test" is recommended as the educatory guiding principle for the execution: But, there is a knowledge question before a topic is broached at all. This affects another candor for the topic.[16] Then follows the input, which is again implemented and tested in the next step. Other success factors are the use of a variety of media, the application of what is learnt as well as a positive and motivating learning environment. Last but not the least is offering VAKOG-specific[17] learning, that is, learning that addresses all senses.

---

[16] For this, please refer to the extremely interesting read, how to learn effectively, by Benedict Carey: Neues Lernen. Warum Faulheit und Ablenkung dabei helfen. Hamburg 2015. In this context, particularly pages 129–60.

[17] In NLP, the perception of reality is described with the help of the senses: visual, auditory, kinaesthetic, olfactory, gustatory.

- **Training follow-up:** Follow-up especially also considers application of what is learnt, as well as coaching, during implementation. A knowledge test is also helpful to ensure that whatever is learnt is ingrained deeply.

As described already, knowledge is built up and also embedded or rehearsed in training—in good training, at least. In any case, a training participant "knows" more after the training than before the training. Even if many things are forgotten again or cannot be "recalled" instantly, new synapses are formed, which can partly be used again if required. Other modes of knowledge building are of an individual type.

Knowledge Building by Reading

If the change involves introduction of a new method or a new system, that is, if it includes a strong element of knowledge building, relevant reading will promote knowledge building. Reading can naturally be part of training, especially in the preparatory phase. However, it can also be used consciously as an individual element in change projects. In case of a cultural change initiative itself, we have used books that describe change dynamics in an easy-to-read and humorous manner, so that the senior management team had already heard of the fundamentals of change at least once in the subsequent workshop.

When a new product is introduced or if the sales department needs a new sales approach, reading—which particularly addresses the naturally analytical employees—is always used. However, it can also lay the foundation for change.

As in training, the following is applicable here: Knowledge can be created by reading a new process, the feature of a new system or a new standard, if the participants are well prepared for the change; when they know what is changed, why and when it is changed and they agree with it in principle.

Knowledge Building by Web-Based Learning

Knowledge is built not just by reading, but also by web-based learning. Webinars and other online formats often go beyond pure reading; they are interactive, can contain films, images, audio formats, texts, quiz, and questionnaires as well as knowledge questions, and are therefore holistic; however, they are usually not in-depth. They can contribute toward building the foundation by being a supporting measure for change. However, unlike reading, online formats frequently require more effort in design and execution. Once they are made, they cannot be changed very well. Therefore, this form of knowledge building is usually only applied in major change measures, where it is clearly outlined what the employee has to learn through the compulsory webinar.

When web-based knowledge building takes effect, it should be very clearly discussed beforehand whether it is about information, inspiration, or explicit learning of new processes, tools, or behaviors.

Knowledge Building by Learning-By-Doing

In everyday life, knowledge is frequently built up, wherein new processes, systems, or tools are briefly introduced and then applied immediately. Naturally, the breadth and depth of this kind of learning is limited and has the inherent risk that something incorrect is practiced and learned. This kind of knowledge building is fully adequate for small changes such as update of an IT program with a few new functionalities. Often in (private) everyday life, it so happens that (complicated) instructions of a new program are not read particularly when the learning of the system is intuitive. Then again, there is the "risk" that not everything is learnt correctly or not learnt fully.

Knowledge Building by Discussions

Sometimes, it is sufficient that all the new things about change are learnt in discussions. It is anyway implicit that employees who have to operate a new system or have to follow a new process exchange views on it, talk about positive and negative experiences, and share their "learnings" with one another. As an accompanying measure, it is also applied consciously especially to ensure that the necessary knowledge is actually present and is understood.

Knowledge Building Through Workshop Formats

In addition to training, workshops of every description accompany the respective change. Whereas training is rather didactic, the workshop opens up a space where a variety of topics relevant to change can be worked upon. The workshop contents and formats show how wide and varied changes can be. From a change perspective, it is important to focus on the questions of the participants. Everything that the employees work out for themselves and what directly docks onto their questions has a far greater probability of being retained and implemented in everyday life. At times, workshops also offer the opportunity to check whether the people concerned are ready at all to consume the new knowledge. Especially when basic questions on change arise on their own within the framework of the workshop ("Why do we need it at all?"), these questions should be given the necessary platform. Ruth Cohn has formulated the disturbance posit in the theme-centered interaction (TZI): "Disturbances take precedence." Sources of disturbance can be internal and external. In change projects, they often pertain to resistance to change, which can assume multicausal manifestations. However, this "disturbance" prevents learning. For this reason, they must be worked on professionally in the workshop.

The workshop moderation plays a decisive role in perceiving the mood with regard to change and also to adapt the flow of the workshop spontaneously, to identify the "knowledge gap," and to orient the contents and flow of the workshop exactly toward it. Spontaneity and creativity do not replace structure and specifications rather presuppose them.

New abilities are learnt in a variety of different ways. First, it is always about knowledge building, but which is already linked with practicing new abilities. Sometimes, practicing and entrenching of new abilities are given too little chance; therefore, they must be dealt with separately over here.

Practicing Abilities

Those who have acquired a driving license very well know the difference between knowledge and ability. Learning is theoretical first and then practical, wherein basic knowledge about road traffic and its rules are taught. This knowledge becomes practical knowledge by driving lessons, and the driving license acquired confirms that the learner driver can exhibit basic knowledge and even basic abilities that allow him to drive the car independently in road traffic.

However, if the new driving license holder decides after the test not to drive any car for 10 years, he might have to start again from the beginning after these 10 years because the decisive phase of practicing the new abilities starts after knowledge building, until they are unconsciously "acquired" and are integrated in everyday life.

The importance of the "ability" is similarly evident in the topic on coaching. A long training in coaching on its own does not qualify the coach to teach every student in a professional and satisfactory manner in every situation. However, application of the knowledge and contemplation of successes and failures will contribute in making the newly acquired behavior of the coach an integral part of his personality and his actions.

Here, both the main components leading to sustained learning of new behaviors are mentioned: application and contemplation. Both actions determine each other: The knowledge acquired must be implemented so that the change becomes sustainable. However, during and after application, it requires stopping and reviewing, refining the new behavior. Contemplation is not to be understood as an intellectual exercise here—even if it can be part of implementation. By contemplation, we mean working in detail on implementation that includes verifying whether the new behavior matches the new standard and deriving measures for improvement as to how the new behavior can be rehearsed.

Application: Practicing Abilities

One of the main tasks of change agents is helping employees to sustainably adopt the new behavior, the new process, the new system application, or the new cultural challenge. As in the case of driving or coaching, it mainly happens by *doing*. The important thing here is that old behavior becomes unattractive and impossible and new behavior becomes attractive and is enabled. If new teams are specially created with new task areas, employees may no longer have the opportunity to work on old themes.[18]

---

[18] Similarly, infrastructure must also support the new behavior.

Moreover, persons affected by the change must have easy access to experts who are always available and happy to answer any queries. Especially during IT implementations, we have frequently observed that the training experts are there ("knowledge"). However, after the initial ability has been imparted, they are already on their way to the next setting. Changes are quick and long-lasting where experts are available on-site and make sure that knowledge becomes ability.

Contemplation: Identifying Improvement Measures

Experts mainly help in identifying the difference to the behavior striven for, deriving improvement measures and supervising their implementation: "Coaching on details" observes what is implemented and what is not in great detail. In the process, it provides tactful support in building and enhancing new abilities.

Case Study

In a culture change project, the leadership style must be adapted, among other things. The "command-and-control" style has been adopted so far. Team meetings consisted of information and "announcements"; a one-way communication, which just allowed one question at the most toward the end. The driving factors for change were first the lack of motivation in employees, and second the lack of implementation strength of the measures of improvement. One subgoal was also changing the style of leadership communication. Behavior that was practiced over decades, which could be described as part of cultural DNA, only changes by multipolar approaches. The part to be described here was in a modified structure of team meetings with a new communication behavior of the executives. The executives were supposed to listen more and moderate, rather than go on talking. This new behavior was discussed extensively in the training and was practiced initially. However, the focus is now on implementing the behavior in everyday life and on making it the new leadership behavior. The natural tendency of every person is to retreat to his comfort zone, especially in stressful situations.

The new behavior supported by extensive infrastructure measures could be taught by experts over several weeks. It was observed and measured in detail how often and which questions were asked, what was the level of the listening skill, and how the self-motivation of employees was incorporated and operationalized. The concrete change potentials were discussed (and also trained in parts) in very regular and very concrete feedback discussions and their implementation was also reviewed. This very specific contemplation and detailed coaching including specific measurement proved to be strong drivers of change. The step from conscious to unconscious competence was taken here— and only it makes change sustainable.

Rehearsing physical and intellectual abilities is only marginally different. But, it is important in any case to identify change potentials as specifically as possible and to practice the new ability in a structured and sustainable manner. Feedback loops play an important role here.

Capacity to Learn and Change

Sometimes, the question as to the ability to learn and change arises both at an individual as well as at an organizational level. Based on biographical constellations, some people have an affinity to change and are ready to learn, whereas others resist change and learning. Organizations (right from team, functional or country organization to international corporations) can also be described as ready or resistant to change and learn, depending on experience and culture. At this point, fewer individual learning resistances should be described because they are a separate topic and are especially relevant in practice; but, they cannot be answered in a pedagogical-educational manner. So, for example, employees of an organization coming from educationally deprived classes may find it rather difficult, from an intellectual viewpoint, to know the details of the so-called SOP. Relevant learning concepts could find a customized solution for it.

Real-world challenges are in analyzing and overcoming limited capacity for learning and changing. As the cause can be manifold at the personal level, we cannot achieve a lot by finding out the cause at an individual level. Therefore, the focus should be on measuring the capacity to learn and change and on deriving measures for overcoming obstacles. The learn-capacity-model can be a tool for it. It is a diagnosis tool that gauges the learning capacity of an organization.

Toolbox

Learn-Capacity-Model

The learning capacity of an organization is examined with the help of the following dimensions:
- Age of persons affected by change
- Retention period at the current place
- Fluctuation of the employees
- Number and intensity of past changes
- Employee engagement
- Management of ideas
- Standards and continuous improvement
- Diversity of the organization (age, gender, nationality, educational background).

Basically, it can be said that: The more flexible an organization is, which can be seen, for example, by the duration for which employees remain in their workplace, the more adaptive it is. At the same time, however, there is the "learning hiccup," which is known to some from the time of test preparation. For the learning to be integrated into life needs time. If a lot is consumed at one go, there comes a "hiccup," that is, time is required to incorporate the learning. If there is a lot of change in organizations and at times uncoordinated too, the capacity of an organization to learn and change is exhausted very soon and the new knowledge has to be applied even before it can be explored.

Coaching and Feedback

As mentioned already, coaching and feedback are central to change programs. Here, coaching has a special significance in the corporate context. Unlike professional business and life coaching, this refers to a form of leadership that galvanizes and enables employees and thereby their own experience can be incorporated. The (philosophical) question as to what is correct coaching should. however, be disregarded here; rather, it makes much more sense to again practically consider the types of coaching and feedback that can be helpful to change. Two models are tried and tested and are applied in many companies: The FUEL[19] (English *fuel* = drive; strengthen) and the GROW[20] model (English *grow* = grow, improve). Both are similar and provide a framework for change agents and executives which allows them to initiate or to intensify behavioral changes in employees.

Toolbox

Fuel

- **Frame the conversation**—give the conversation a frame
  The first step is to give the conversation a frame: The objective, the process, and the desired end result of the conversation are thematized.
- **Understand the current state**—taking a closer look at the current situation
  In the second step, the current situation is studied closely from the perspective of the person receiving coaching to better understand the problem or the reason for the conversation or discussion.
- **Explore the desired state**—examining the desired change
  In the third step, different proposals for solution are considered to find out what a successful solution can look like.
- **Lay out a success plan**—describing the success plan
  In the last step, clear milestones are fixed, which are necessary to arrive at the decided result.

---

[19] Zenger, J.H., and K. Stinnett. 2010. *The Extraordinary Coach: How the Best Leaders Help Others Grow.* New York.
[20] Whitmore, J. 2009. *Coaching for Performance: GROWing Human Potential and Purpose—The Principles and Practice of Coaching and Leadership.* London, Boston.

The models are similar and our experience tells us that it is less important to follow the individual steps of a model precisely than it is to understand the underlying principles, as they are important for every behavioral change. The "coach" plays a pivotal role here. He helps in unmasking the inner and outer resistances, in modeling the new behavior and then even in implementing it.

Toolbox

Grow

- **Goal**—determining the objective
  The first step is examining the desired behavioral change and fixing a clear and measurable objective of success.
- **Reality**—examining the reality
  The second step examines, as clear and free of judgment as possible, the present reality with regard to the desired change.
- **Options**—studying the options
  The third step looks for as many choices as possible to achieve the objective, whereby the number is more important than the quality.
- **Will/Way forward**—examining the intentions/the next steps
  The last step deals with choosing an option from among many and deliberating as to what can help in achieving this goal.

Therefore, the fundamental principles of a change coaching comprise:

- Understanding the present reality
- Gaining clarity about the change to be achieved
- Specifying verifiable steps with regard to the change

If these steps are applied empathically, a steep learning curve is achieved with high probability.

Learning in Change

Willingness and ability to learn are indispensible in change. However change appears, the old must always be unlearned, and the new must be learnt. Learning itself usually is a big motivational factor as people want to progress. An important question here is how this learning process can be managed best. For this, we shall first consider Mumford and Kolb's learning style as well as Kolb's learning cycle. Finally, learning in trainings should be examined as almost every change includes a training component. The question as to what effective training looks like arises here.

Learning as Motivator

A lot of literature is available on the topic of what motivation is, how it is created, and what role it plays for learning, which cannot be discussed here in detail. Cook and Artino provide a very good overview of it.[21]

Basically, motivation can be seen in the attitude of willing to achieve an objective, and in the process of starting and executing this journey. A closely related aspect is the topic of employee engagement. Inclusion in decision-making processes, personal value contribution, attention to health and well-being, and finally the possibility to develop further are identified and defined as key drivers for employee engagement, in addition to appreciation, good relations with superiors and colleagues, as well as meaningful work.[22] But, developing further or enhancing oneself mainly means to learn. Therefore, support in the personal development of employees cannot be rated high enough and should be consciously used in specific change projects.

> ### Case Study
>
> A company's warehouse always suffered from a negative atmosphere, and there was also high fluctuation, negative results, and mainly

---

21   Cook, D.A., and A.A. Artino. 2016. "Motivation to Learn: An Overview of Contemporary Theories." *Medical Education* 50, no. 10, pp. 997–1014.
22   Robinson, D., S. Perryman, and S. Hayday. 2004. "The Drivers of Employee Engagement." Report 403, Institute for Employment Studies.

employee motivation was almost zero; this was reflected in a high percentage of employee sickness and vacancies as well as low performance. Our change project dealt with the question: "What does the best day look like?" In their responses, employees described mostly consistent aspects such as recognition by superiors, enough breaks, proper order, and fair behavior of colleagues. But, a recurring element was: "We could contribute in becoming better." This contribution comprised minor process-related and other workflow changes, which led to increased performance and also increased motivation or stronger engagement.

Learning something new and enhancing the self through it is a motivation element in CM that just cannot be underestimated. In the process, the various learning styles illustrated in a paradigmatic manner by Honey and Mumford must be considered here.[23]

Learning Styles According to Honey and Mumford

Honey and Mumford have described four types of learning, which should be considered while planning trainings (Figure 5.1). When such learning styles are recognized, their application can become a major driver of change:

- The *Activist* learns by doing. He will learn less from a lecture and more from role play and active involvement.
- The *Reflector* learns by observation and contemplation. He will learn less under pressure and more from distance and contemplation.
- The *Theorist* learns through models, analyses, and concepts. He will learn less in unclear or even in emotional situations and more by structure and reduction in complexity.

---

[23] Honey, P. 1986. "Alan Mumford: The Manual of Learning Styles." *Peter Honey Associates*, Maidenhead.

1. Concrete
Experience

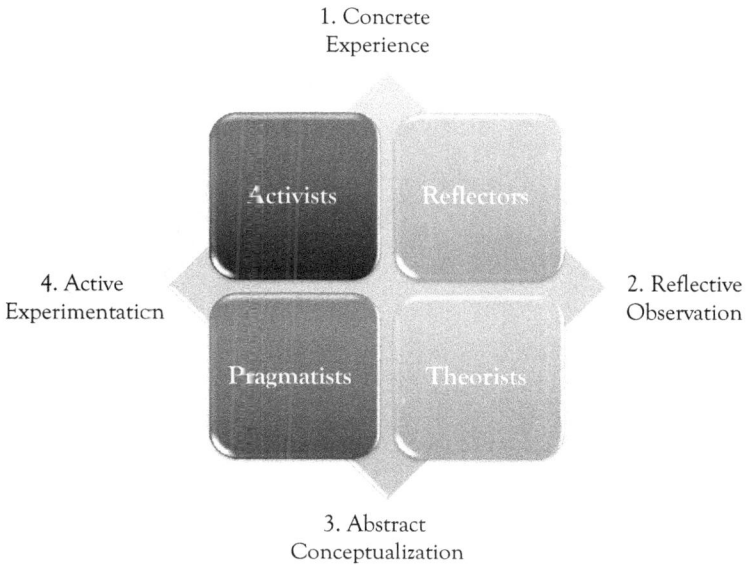

4. Active
Experimentation

2. Reflective
Observation

3. Abstract
Conceptualization

Figure 5.1 *Learning styles according to Honey and Mumford*

- The *Pragmatist* learns by implementing new ideas. He will learn less in theoretical situations, which do not have any practical relevance, and more through imitation and experimentation.

Kolb's Learning Cycle

Kolb's learning cycles related to the model described earlier.

More than 30 years ago, David Kolb (1983) developed the learning model, which comprises four different learning styles on the one hand and one four-phase cycle on the other (Figure 5.2).[24]

Just like Honey and Mumford, Kolb sees a natural preference of the individual for a particular learning style, but describes in another manner. Kolb first differentiates between process and perception. The process continuum describes how we approach a task (observe or do), whereas the

---

[24] The following is mainly based on: McLeod, S. A. 2017. *Kolb—learning styles.* For this, see also: www.simplypsychology.org/learning-kolb.html [Date of access: 26.01.2019]. Also refer to Daniel Kolb. 1983. *Experiential Learning.* New Jersey.

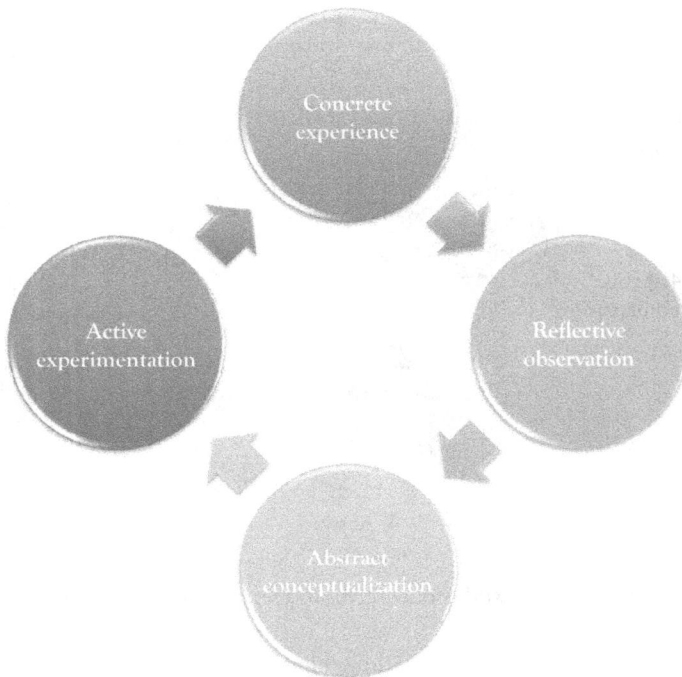

Figure 5.2 *Kolb's learning cycle*

perception continuum describes how we respond to something (emotionally or rationally). So then, the learning style is made up of a combination of two elements (Figure 5.3).

Kolb describes the learning styles: diverging, assimilating, converging, and accommodating as follows:

- **Diverging** (differing)—sensitive people, who would rather observe and gather information, are emotional and person-oriented, prefer learning through group work.
- **Assimilating** (adapting)—people, who think logically and conceptually, who are interested in abstract concepts and logical theories, prefer learning through reading and listening.
- **Converging** (merging)—facts-and solutions-oriented people, who are less interested in interpersonal aspects and are more decisive, prefer learning through practical application.

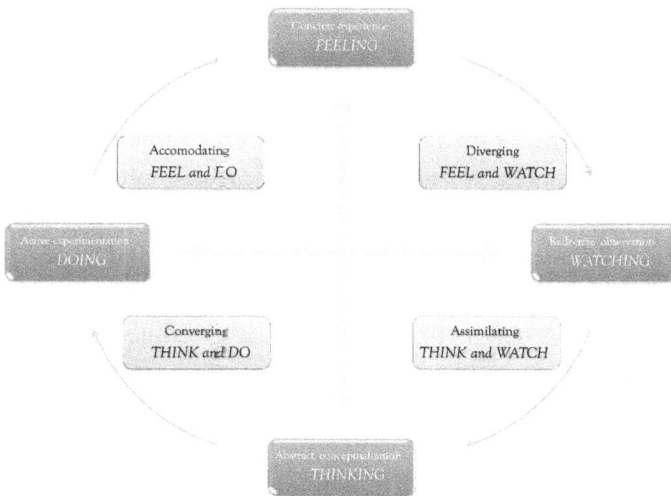

Figure 5.3 *Kolb's learning phases*

- **Accommodating** (obliging)—intuitive, practical, and experience-oriented people, such as challenges and implementations, depend on their instinct and prefer learning through emulation.

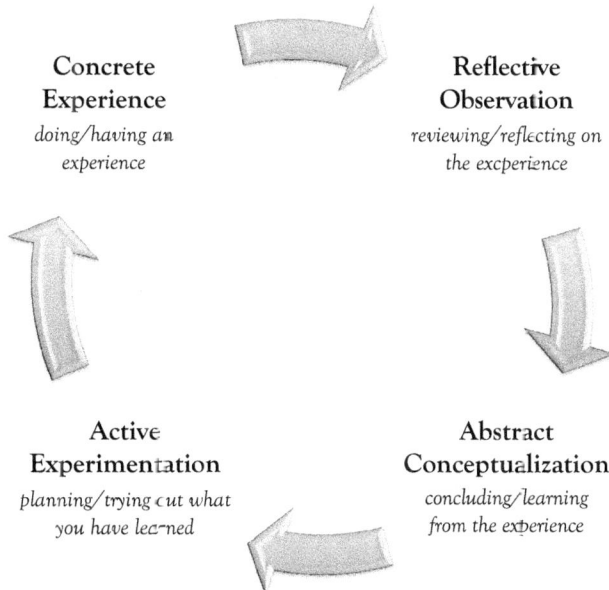

Figure 5.4 *Kolb's learning cycles*

Kolb's four-phase cycle describes the process of learning: The learner starts with a (new) experience, reflects on it, draws conclusions, and implements them. This learning cycle has practical implications for change programs: Instead of setting up a new process, a new product, or a new system for employees, it is better to give them a new experience, letting them reflect or contemplate this experience, also draw their own conclusions, and derive practical implications from it (Figure 5.4). This experience can be obtained with the help of various methods and different exercises. You can find one sample exercise below.

Case Study

Exercise: "Change yourself"

The moderator requests participants to make pairs. The partners then stand facing each other and one person receives the assignment of changing something about self, while the other person has to turn around. If person A has changed something in self, person B must turn back again and try to find out what the person in front of him has changed. This assignment is repeated 5 to 10 times. In most cases, it becomes clear upon reflection that participants initially only thought in "less mode": Removing the pullover, shirt, watch, belt, and so on; abstraction reflects that actual change is also perceived in the "less mode." The practical implication deliberates on how a change in view can happen: Difference does not automatically indicate less, but under certain circumstances, more or at least even "different."

Learning in Trainings

Learning in changes happens in trainings in particular. What should be the structure of trainings so that learning is also effective? The main features of effective training should be presented below in brief. For this, individual, training, and organization-specific characteristics are described.[25]

Individual Traits of the Trainee

First of all, the character traits of the trainee are important. They include self-monitoring, self-efficacy, enthusiasm, and so on. Also working knowledge that comprises knowledge, abilities, experience, and finally motivation is also important. The motivation to participate in training (pre-motivation) and also the motivation to apply the learning after the training (post-motivation) are crucial. Therefore, for the training to be highly effective, it is important to carry out a pre-scan of the candidates. It is not easy with the personality traits; the working knowledge can be more objective and the motivation can be examined in assessment. What has always been done to have the correct participants in training: The effectiveness of training increases demonstrably if the individual traits of the trainees are included.

Training Features

In addition to the actual training features such as content, design and delivery, pre-and post-training elements should also be taken into

---

[25] The following ideas are inspired by these authors, among others: Alvarez, K., E. Salas, C.M. Garofano. 2004. "An Integrated Model of Training Evaluation and Effectiveness." *Human Resource Development Review* 3, pp. 385–416; Baldwin, T.T., and J.K. Ford. 1988. "Transfer of Training: A Review and Directions for Future Research." *Personnel Psychology* 41, no. 1, pp. 63–105; Cheng, E.W., and I. Hampson. 2008. "Transfer of Training: A Review and New Insights." *International Journal of Management Reviews* 10, no. 4, pp. 327–41; Grossman, R., and E. Salas. 2011. "The Transfer of Training: What Really Matters." *International Journal of Training and Development* 15, pp. 103–20; Velada, R., and C. Antonio, J.W. Michel, B.D. Lyons, and M.J. Kavanagh. 2007. "The Effects of Training Design, Individual Characteristics and Work Environment on Transfer of Training." *International Journal of Training and Development* 11, pp. 282–94; Wentland, D. 2003. "The Strategic Training of Employees Model: Balancing Organizational Constraints and Training Content." *Advanced Management Journal* 68, pp. 56–63.

consideration: A requirement analysis must be conducted before training. There should be coaching or mentoring after training to make sure that training is transferred.

Organization-Specific Features

The most frequently mentioned organization-specific features that increase the effectiveness of training are management support, infrastructure (e.g., to also implement training contents later), and the engagement of the organization (e.g., reference to the organization strategy).

In every major change project, there is something new to learn which is conveyed in training. Considering the features mentioned will help in improving the effectiveness of training.

Overcoming Resistances

In case of stakeholder management, the core element of activities lies in working on resistances at the *human* level. But even *structural* resistances can interfere with the effectiveness of change initiatives, so that work needs to be done on overcoming them:

- Most of the change projects take place under time pressure. Often, the time window is not very large, especially for CM initiatives. Good time management, however, is very important because priorities are specified here and change managers need influencing and convincing capabilities to highlight the importance of CM.
- Very often, there is too little training or the quality of training is not good enough. With regard to training quality, the importance of the post-training phase needs to be emphasized here once again. Training must also be supplemented by supporting activities.
- Change practitioners with very little training, who can conduct workshops, take interviews, make assessments, or can coach, are the norm and not the exception, as per our experience. The first task of the persons responsible for change is to

ensure that the workload for the commissioned trainers does not increase disproportionately, but is prioritized accordingly. Prioritizing and focusing help in effective controlling of the workload on experts.

- Sometimes, there is no established feedback or monitoring structure. Therefore, too little is learnt from errors, or rather, continuous improvement is still not an element of the new culture.
- Finally, there is a continual and overall lack of financial support. As in case of all projects, it is necessary to balance input and output.

Summary

- Leadership is an ability that can be learnt, which is mainly distinguished by being able to connect with people, displaying emotional intelligence and practicing mindfulness.
- It is important to build up knowledge before abilities can be practiced.
- Learning can be learnt.
- Coaching and feedback are key abilities for every change.

CHAPTER 6

How MIC Is Applied

In the male-dominated business world, thinking has been more linear and not circular over several years, and largely even today. Project management methods illustrate this conceptual approach, if they classically contain a sequence of steps formed at the start of the project (plan), then to monitor the project control to finally reach a conclusion. Be it three, five, or six steps, at the core it is always about these main steps. In recent times, there is an increasing number of other project methods that pursue a circular approach to some extent.

CM differs from PM to the extent that interventions usually cannot be handled as in case of project milestones. When persons affected by change do not need to be convinced of the change any more, one should not start with why workshops, whereas these workshops can be the first step if change is not accepted in the organization.

Approaches that address the mindset or the process of Design Thinking are helpful for CM: One always starts with the challenge and tries to define the problem. PM is usually solution-oriented. In Design Thinking and in CM, one first attempts to understand the problem in-depth. If, for example, the causes for resistance are not understood and appreciated sufficiently, a hasty solution will not lead to any success because employees will not feel understood. Even in the problem-solving phase (ideation), in design thinking, one tries to think obliquely and broadly instead of acting in haste. Finally, prototyping is an indication of the temporary nature of solutions. If employees are not presented with *the* solution, *the* new process, *the* new organization, but rather *one* option for that, and if they have the option to contribute to the solution, then there is considerable increase in acceptance Finally, the circular principle in CM proves itself time and again. As the emotional states of employees can change in the course of the change, it is often advisable to "return" to the topics and to once again thematize change dimensions that have already been worked upon.

In practice, however, it has been seen that top management finds it extremely difficult to accept this circular, often spontaneous, creative, and re-active, not pro-active approach. Therefore, it is very helpful to select a linear approach to create higher acceptance for CM itself. However, change professionals are aware that this linear approach is relative and the individual elements cannot be simply "worked upon" such as the to-do's of a project list; rather, they can be delayed or even repeated.

Therefore, the PACE model should be presented hereafter. PACE stands for Prepare, Analyze, Carry, and Effect. It takes into consideration the principal requirements of each change project and is therefore flexible enough to be adapted to the project with regard to size, type, and management of the respective change. This linear focus and flexible circularity enables high tempo (pace) of change.

The first step (*Prepare*) is understanding and defining the change. It is typically about the team, the management, the *What* and *Why* of change.

The second step (*Analyze*) outlines a holistic diagnosis: Here, it is about understanding the *Effects* of change on the concerned persons and deriving *Measures* for generating higher acceptance for the change.

Finally, the measures are implemented by a multitude of initiatives (*Carry* into execution). Subsequently, sustained entrenchment in the organizational culture is ensured (*Effect* sustainability).

Prepare—Preparation Phase

Project Team

In case of medium to large change projects and programs, there is one project or change team to be formed which must coordinate. Experience tells us that the members go through the phases of Tuckman's phase model. With the knowledge of these phases, loss of friction can be reduced or avoided by appropriate measures at the time of building the team by forming an effective TEAM:

- **Targets** of the project—the project objectives must be defined: What is it about, what is the task of the team, what is to be achieved?
- **Efficiency** of the team—the efficiency of the team must be defined: How does the team work together, how do they coordinate, what is the definition of success, how do they communicate, how are decisions made and implemented?
- **Allocation** of tasks—the person-specific tasks must be defined: Who does what, who takes over which task, and what exactly is expected from that?
- **Mastery** of stress—stress interventions must be defined: What happens in stressful situations, how are disagreements dealt with, how can corrective measures be defined and implemented beforehand, what are the solutions to relieve stress?

Toolbox

Forming a TEAM

- Set *Targets*/objectives for the team.
- Define *Efficiency* of the team processes.
- Discuss *Allocation*/assignment of tasks and roles.
- *Mastery* of stress: Define how stress is to be dealt with.

Senior Management Support

A, if not *the*, decisive success factor for every change is the support of (top) management team.

In the preparation time of the change project, there should be clarity about the type of support of (top) executives. Sometimes, it is not clear as to who the initiator (sponsor) is or there are inconsistencies about the necessary support of the sponsor. This is easily evident in the readiness to invest time and resources in the project. The project must be stopped if this support is not there or if it is not clear. Then it will not be successful and continuing the process will only consume resources. If the sponsor is not one with the decision-making authority (in case of inconsistencies, and even generally), then a (program) manager must be designated who holds this decision-making power and who is also available for the project and for regular meetings.

The fact that the sponsor extends unlimited support for the change project and not his senior management team (SMT) is more the norm than an exception. Ensuring this support is one of the first and foremost tasks of the change manager. It includes, on the one hand, giving the respective managers time according to the emotional change curve so that they can make up their mind for the change. On the other hand, gentle pressure needs to be applied so that it becomes clear that there is only a "hop or top": Either the project must be supported with full commitment or it should be given up completely. Good CM is evident not least in coaching the SMT in order to attract all members for the change, as far as possible.

Guiding Coalition

"Guiding coalition" (GC) includes employees from all levels who support the change and who are very influential at their level (the so-called opinion leaders). The concept of GC should be shared with the SMT right from the beginning so that potential members can be found from the start. The best thing is to ask the managers themselves to form this team. They know their people and know pretty quickly who will naturally support the change and who is accepted by the colleagues.

The GC is an instrument of leadership and communication, and the members act as ambassadors of change: They bring the message of the latest considerations, decisions, forthcoming changes to their colleagues, and conversely act as a mouthpiece for their colleagues. Therefore, management of the GC is a sensitive issue, which needs to be managed jointly by the sponsor and the people in-charge of change. When a trustful relationship has evolved in due course of time, the GC acts like a catalyst. This results in rapid fundamental acceptance. However, a poorly managed GC can also have the exact opposite effect if there is no honesty and truth: Resistance for change can become so great that the GC becomes an anti-GC which hinders change.

Explaining the What of the Change

As described earlier,[1] every change includes the explanation related to what the change exactly entails.

Two elements need to be highlighted at this point: Both, the organizational as well as the human aspect of change must be described here as minutely as possible.

- **The organizational aspect of change must be defined clearly**
  - In case of a new software implementation, it needs to be exactly described as to what is to be implemented, when, and what are the technical effects of the change.
  - In case of a reorganization, the new structures, the new team composition, the new leadership structure, new responsibilities, and elimination of tasks are precisely described.
  - When new processes are introduced, both, what the (old) existing processes are all about as well as what the (new) processes to be introduced are all about, are described in detail.
  - In case of cultural changes, which cultural elements change and how they change, for example, leadership principles or engagement initiatives, are also described in detail.
  - Whatever be the change, the leading question always is: What changes—and what does not change? Both should be written down and visualized.

The influence of this change on the persons involved must be highlighted, in addition to the organizational aspects.

- **The human aspect of change must be defined clearly**
  The leading question here is: What is the effect of the respective change on whom and who can conversely form the change?

---

[1] Cf. Section "The What—Sensitize for Change" (Chapter 3).

Change must be analyzed in-depth before being able to answer these questions in detail. In this phase of change, it is sufficient when an initial understanding can be gained of the effect of change on the persons involved and of the executives on the change. For example, introduction of new software can cause the work processes of employees to fundamentally change or that new reporting structures can form new team compositions and new tasks.

Working on the Why

As has been shown earlier,[2] the description of the reason for change is a decisive factor for the project to be successful.

In this phase of the project, this *Why* cannot be specifically elaborated in-depth and for all stakeholders. Nevertheless, it is important to describe an initial global *Why*, which is as concise and easy to communicate as possible (maximum one sentence).

Gaining an Overview of Stakeholders

This refers to gaining an overview of all those people affected by the change. This can be linked with the deliberation as to how to communicate best with which group (Figure 6.1).

On the one hand, groups can be formed with respect to functions or the respective change: In the process, a group is formed comprising employees affected similarly by change.

On the other hand, an initial assessment can be made with regard to the size of the respective group, whereby groups less affected by the change can be communicated with in the same way, regardless of whether the groups are large or small or even individual persons.

---

[2]   Cf. Section "The Why—Wishes and Needs" (Chapter 3).

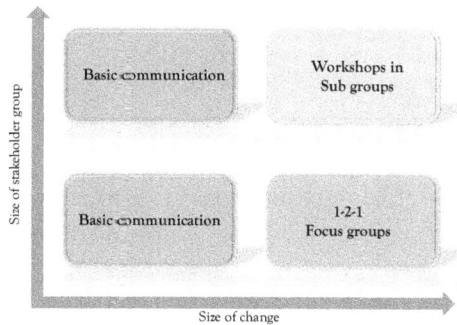

Figure 6.1 *Communication matrix*

Analyze—Diagnostic Phase

Once the contents of change have been examined in the preparation phase and the framework of change could be determined, it is now time for in-depth analysis as to who will be affected and how by the change and what measures can be derived to help the affected persons to adapt to the change and to actively aid in designing it.

It is important to consider that collection of data, carrying out surveys and so on, basically analysis as such, already induces change: Only neutral data is never collected and analyzed; rather, analysis as such influences change. Therefore, in this section of the project, it is particularly important to consider not only the type of data, but also *how* it has been collected. Just as rapport is the basis of every instance of effective coaching, similarly trust forms the basis of every change. Therefore, the change managers will not just pose questions to employees out of the blue, but will sensitively transform the affected persons into participants at diverse levels and—if possible and opportune—involve them in the questions themselves.

Diagnosis of Effects of Change

There are a number of tools and methods at hand for diagnosing a change. Only those areas to be specifically considered will be shown here. Depending on the change, the data concerning employees and also existing data are examined first, then—depending on the change—surveys or stakeholder interviews can be designed and focus groups can be created.

Data

Depending on the magnitude of change, corresponding data sets are available with regard to leadership, engagement, sickness level, turnover, age, company affiliation, diversity, and so on.

Old data related to culture can help in deducing how leadership in general is accepted and what is the engagement level of employees. Even the sickness level and particularly the turnover data indicate the (leadership) culture. Age of the employee or duration of service in the company, diversity of nationality or other public data references to innovative capability, and readiness to change can be there mainly in companies with longer tradition. But here, the change manager must appreciate that time and again there can be distortions in data collection and evaluation. Thus, long association with the company cannot necessarily be equated with resistance to innovation; on the contrary, it can mean an adeptness to change.

The (quantitative) data must be qualitatively verified in any case.

Surveys

Both digital as well as analog surveys are possible, depending on the culture and experience of the organization, and also depending on how easy or difficult it is to answer the questions. If surveys are too long and too complicated, they will not bring the desired information.

The design of the surveys must be well thought out and must be discussed. It is also recommended that the so-called baseline be drawn; that is, an initial survey with respect to fundamental topics, which can be replicated, can be repeated in the course of change and can be carried out once again especially toward the end.

Surveys can be designed according to the main categories of successful CM, so that the initial change initiatives can ensue from the result.

Interviews

Formal and informal interviews can be conducted with individual persons. It is recommended that structured interviews be conducted with executives. A questionnaire is drawn up just as in case of surveys, whereby the interviews consist of qualitative and open questions, rather than quantitative and closed questions. The advantage of this type of interview is that nuances can be captured and the questions can also be deviated from if other important topics start from the conversation.

As regards content, the questions and their structure result from the respective change. Besides the understanding of change (what, why, where), prior experiences as well as perceived support of various stakeholder groups can also be questioned.

Focus groups

While interviews are usually aimed at individual persons, focus groups are made up of representative members of the organization. Here, it is important to consider *how* potential participants are invited. The invitation in itself is part of the change narrative and initiates change. Therefore, in a verbal invitation by a person of trust, it is explained to the potential addressees in more than one sentence what the focus group is all about, why they have been invited, and what is expected of them.

The structure of focus groups can differ as regards content. A guided, semi-written discussion under the headings *Current state–Future state* and possible subthemes: *I–My Team–My Superiors–My Surroundings* has proven itself. It concerns gathering current pain points as well as possible proposals for solution, whereby the proposals for solution cannot often be implemented directly. However, they can specify a direction as to how CM can support the concerned employees.

All results of the quantitative and qualitative diagnoses merge in one complete overview. Focus areas, similarities and contradictions, questions and other observations are cumulated and visualized here once again. Measures can be derived from it, which can then be implemented in the phase of implementation.

Toolbox

Diagnostic Tools

- Surveys
- Interviews
- Focus groups

Definition of Measures

In "normal" projects, the measures form the so-called road map; an overview of individual actions, which are executed one after the other according to the milestones. Caution is advised here in a two-fold manner in change projects. On the one hand, the development of measures is based on a diagnosis, which always includes a subjective shade. On the other hand, change projects are dynamic; so that planned measures that may make sense at the start of a project can also start to look obsolete after a few weeks.

But, what should appear or broaden in any case is a good overview of the concerned stakeholders as well as a "temperature check" related to the question as to which group is most likely to resist, where is support to be expected most, and what the direction of change could be.

These measures are as diverse as every change is different. Therefore, at this point, designing possible stereotyped measures, which would appear to be completely different in practice, is avoided. Instead, in "carry into execution," the implementation phase shows which fundamental principles should be applied in change at this point.

Carry into Execution—Implementation Phase

In the implementation phase, principally all elements of the MIC model are important. All three levels must be worked on, whereby the sequence arises from the project itself. This flexibility is what makes the application of the model successful. A rigid, sequential execution of individual approaches could even jeopardize the project's success.

Over and above it, there are principles and elements which are important in every change situation and which should be shown here.

Change Communication

It is a common misunderstanding that CM can be equated with change communication. At the same time, communication is very important in every change project. How communication can be established and can also succeed has been described in detail in the *What* part (see the section "The What—Sensitize for Change" in Chapter 3). But at this point, it needs to be emphasized once again that the responsibility of communication must act in close coordination with the PM and CM. Here, the communication responsibility will always pay attention to a dialogical communication with Input and Output.

The creation of a change story can once again help in formulating and visualizing the big questions of *What*, *Why*, and *Where* for stakeholders.

Training and Coaching Change Agents

The larger an organization in which change is carried out, the more employees are needed who are trained in implementing individual elements on the path of change, starting from workshops, communication tasks, and trainings up to complex organizational or infrastructure adjustments. As employees are part of the organization, there is another aspect to them: They can have a major influence on the organization just like participants in the GC.

The training of change agents will directly orient itself to change and also to address the MIC model, dealing with resistance and role-specific abilities, in addition to the fundamentals of CM. Here, the change team plays the role of training the change agents (continuously) on the one hand, and coaching them on-the-job on the other hand.

Quick Wins (Proto Typing)

Mainly in the first phase of the emotional change curve, the participants wonder whether the change will actually take place. Many a time, larger companies have loudly announced change; and what has happened— nothing. This experience results in a mood of wait and watch, which even retards the willingness and the ability to change of committed employees. The so-called Quick Wins, on the one hand, highlight the sincerity of change in the implementation mechanism and, on the other hand, convince procrastinators.

Case Study

New workplace models were discussed in an organization unit: Open space models should develop from old, classic two-room models,

usually sealed by a closed door. Instead of introducing these through-
out the organization, open office space with innovative design was
created for a small number of employees. Thus, the first positive experiences could be collected, and inhibitions could also be reduced by
visualization and relatable communication.

According to the nature of things, Quick Wins have not yet covered
the entire change; however, they do contribute fundamentally to the
urgency of change.

In design thinking, it is very important to keep asking the customer
or the user whether the finished product is what the customer expected.
The linear process of product creation per se is interrupted circularly,
for example, also by the fact that a prototype is built at an early stage,
which does not depict all the characteristics of the target product, but
conveys the impression of the direction in which it should proceed. Even
if the change theme is not about introducing a new product, the attitude
behind prototyping is not dissimilar to Quick Win: It is about giving the
participants an experience of the future.

Workshops

The classical method of implementation transfer comprises workshops, in
which the individual elements of change method can be applied. Regardless of whether a WIIFM should be formulated or executives should be
prepared for their task, the format will usually be that of a workshop.
There are various options as well as tips and tricks for designing such
workshops expediently and successfully. Explaining it is outside the scope
of this book. But, there is also a large amount of useful literature.

Summary: Making Change Noticeable

The urgency of change can be perceived when it is implemented at all
professional and functional levels of the company. Continuous communication, role model function of leadership, Quick Wins, implementation of subprojects, involvement of employees, sounding boards, focus
groups, and so on must become the fabric of everyday life.

Effect Sustainability—Sustainable Entrenchment

Changes are considered to be successful in a sustained manner when the entire organization concerned adapts to the change, when new roles are clarified and rehearsed, when the progress of the project can be verified and corrective measures can be derived and implemented, and when the success of the project is evaluated and documented.

Adapting the Organization

As discussed in Chapter 4, the organization must be adapted to the change in case of some changes. In restructuring measures especially, but also in other projects, the extent to which the "organizational setup" matches the "to-be-state" or supports the desired change must be verified. Our experience tells us that parts of the organization are adapted, but there is no overall picture. The leading question here is: Which other as yet unconsidered elements, which probably were not in focus so far, but could influence the success of change, should be adapted with respect to the change? So, for example, in case of a large-scale IT implementation, the organization structure may have been adapted, whereas the ground office situation does not depict the new team and cooperation structure any more.

Adapting Roles If Necessary

Also, new roles may have been designated, but have not been completely "fulfilled." On the one hand, employees may be dissatisfied with their new role, may not feel confident, or may remain reluctant for some other reasons. On the other hand, some roles cannot have been correctly adapted as yet or employees may not have been correctly trained for their role. In any case, the extent to which employees implement the change in their (new) role needs to be verified.

Ensuring Health Checks in Infrastructure

Directly *before* implementation is completed, verification intervals are agreed upon wherein all elements of change are analyzed with regard to their sustained implementation. Surveys or change-readiness-formats are available here as they depict all levels of change.

Evaluation and Documentation

It is not self-evident that the progress and success of a project is measured continuously and is also documented accordingly. CM wants to make changes sustainable. Sustainable CM gains by continuous evaluation to formulate "lessons learned" in that manner: Which areas have been covered already, which are still open, what was successful, what needs to be readjusted?—these are only some of the topics to be dealt with. On the one hand documentation is important for communication of the change, and on the other hand for the continuous learning curve of the project team. As changes are rather more than less and often enough either help or overlap, documented activities, results, and learning outcomes help in addressing the next change project in a better and more effective manner.

Change is sustained not least by including all dimensions of the MIC model in planning and by carrying out relevant activities.

Epilogue

No matter where the numbers may come from showing that 70 percent of change projects are not successful,[1] our experience tells us that change projects can be implemented successfully if they take the MIC structure into consideration. Nevertheless, changes remain challenging and exciting. At the moment, I can observe two conflicting trends, which I want to present with some intensity to explain the poles:

On the one hand, there is an aversion to change. People are sick and tired of always having to change and look for stability in all directions: changing nothing if possible, ducking their heads when the storm of change is drawing near and hoping that it does not wreak a tsunami of ravages. This attitude easily causes one to become passive, happily ignorant, or depressive. But, it also reflects a helplessness with regard to many questions as to how to best evade the constant changes entailed by modern, everyday life.

On the other hand, there are change promoters who do not get tired of preaching that change is the new constant, connected with the underlying pressure: "Do you want to be modern and a player of tomorrow who must be taken seriously? Then become a part of the fast and furious change party." This often striking opinion reminds me of the statement of a young woman where she said that she could never understand why there were overweight people, though it was clear enough that one had to take care of oneself. Let's disregard this hardly empathic statement for now. But it again shows how diverse the reasons against change can be, and how well-meaning advice like "Just do it differently" can be of little help. But some people find it rather difficult to deal with changes because of personal, political, or cultural experiences. Not everyone knows

---

[1] For this, please refer to the quite fascinating study by Prof. Dr. Ali Mohammad Mosadeghrad of the reasons why change programs (still) fail: Mosadeghrad, A.M. 2014. Maryam Ansarian: Why do organisational change programmes fail? *International Journal of Strategic Change Management* 5, no. 3, pp. 189–218.

that being given wise advice alone does not make people change faster. Change needs a lot more than just a motivated attitude, as we have seen in this book.

The positive message is: One can learn how to deal positively with change. It is in fact possible to view changes not as an enemy, but rather as a friend; to discover potential and not horror in them. As with every challenge that life throws at us, one needs to show the readiness to embark on such a journey.

If this book has made a small contribution in encouraging people to embrace changes constructively and to manage them professionally, it has achieved its objective.

Appendix

Overview of the Tools

H × S = E	Hard multiplied by soft factors equals the result.
3-C-Communication: clear, consistent, comprehensive	Good change communication is clear, consistent, and comprehensive.
One-line-statement	The content of change is described in one line. The process leading to this statement is decisive.
In or out	All elements belonging to change are marked in a box, those that do not belong to change are marked outside the box, and those that need to be discussed are marked on the box frame.
Focus groups	Horizontally and vertically mixed groups (different hierarchical levels and various attitudes toward change) describe their experience of loss and formulate possible positive effects of change.
Team building	Clarify objectives, processes, and roles

Stakeholder Analysis

Stakeholder	Measurement of resistance	Reasons (personal, political, cultural)	WIIFM	Visualization of the system	Influence strategy

What-If Tool

In the workshop format, employees describe the future, particularly from a behavioral and quality perspective.

SCS Tool

- Start: Which behavior should be started to achieve the vision?
- Continue: Which behavior should be continued to achieve the vision?
- Stop: Which behavior should be stopped to achieve the vision?

Change Story

The history of change is visualized taking the following questions into consideration:

- What was the past like?
- What was good and may thus be appreciated accordingly?
- What should change and why?
- What does the future look like?
- How can every concerned person contribute toward a positive future?
- What does leadership promise and what does it expect?
- What are the next steps?

Competence Matrix

	Incompetence		
Unconscious	Unconscious incompetence	Conscious incompetence	Conscious
	Unconscious competence	Conscious competence	
	Competence		

Learn-Capacity-Model

The learning capacity of the organization is examined with the help of the following dimensions:

- Age of persons affected by change
- Retention period at the current place
- Turnover of the employees

- Number and intensity of past changes
- Employee engagement
- Management of ideas
- Standards and continuous improvement
- Diversity of the organization (age, gender, nationality, educational background)

FUEL (developed by John Zenger and Kathleen Stinnet)

- *Frame the conversation*—give the conversation a frame
  The first step is to give the conversation a frame: The objective, the process, and the desired result of the conversation are thematized.
- *Understand the current state*—taking a closer look at the current situation
  In the second step, the current situation is studied closely from the perspective of the person receiving coaching to better understand the problem or the reason for the conversation or discussion.
- *Explore the desired state*—examining the desired change
  In the third step, different proposals for solution are considered to find out what a successful solution can look like.
- *Lay out a success plan*—describing the success plan
  In the last step, clear milestones are fixed, which are necessary to arrive at the decided result.

Grow (developed by John Witmore, Max Landsberg, and others)

- **Goal**—determining the objective
  The first step is examining the desired behavioral change and fixing a clear and measurable objective of success.
- **Reality**—examining the reality
  The second step examines, as clearly and free of judgment as possible, the present reality with regard to the desired change.
- **Options**—studying the options

The third step looks for as many choices as possible to achieve the objective, whereby the number is more important than the quality.

- **Will/way forward**—examining the intentions/the next steps
  The last step deals with choosing an option from among many and deliberating as to what can help in achieving this goal.

Forming a TEAM

- Set **T**argets/objectives for the team.
- Define **E**fficiency of the team processes.
- Discuss **A**llocation/assignment of tasks and roles.
- **M**astery of stress: Define how stress is to be dealt with.

Diagnostic Tools

- Surveys
- Interviews
- Focus groups

References

Alvarez, K., E. Salas, and C.M. Garofano. 2004. "An Integrated Model of Training Evaluation and Effectiveness." *Human Resource Development Review* 3, pp. 385–416.

Baldwin, T.T., and J.K. Ford. 1988. "Transfer of Training: A Review and Directions for Future Research." *Personnel Psychology* 41, pp. 63–105.

Carey, B. 2014. *Neues Lernen. Warum Faulheit und Ablenkung dabei helfen.* Hamburg 2015.

Cheng, E.W.L., and I. Hampson. 2008. "Transfer of Training: A Review and New Insights" *International Journal of Management Reviews* 10, pp. 327–41.

Cook, D.A., and A. Artino 2016. "Motivation to Learn: An Overview of Contemporary Theories." *Medical Education* 50, no. 10, pp. 997–1014. Available online at: https://ncbi.nlm.nih.gov/pmc/articles/PMC5113774/ (accessed on January 8. 2019).

Covey, S. 1989/2004. *7 Habits of Highly Effective People.* New York.

Drucker, P. 1993. *Concept of the Corporation,* p. xvii. New York.

Goleman, D. 1996. "Emotional Intelligence." *Why It Can Matter More than IQ.* London.

Grossman, R., and E. Salas. 2011. "The Transfer of Training: What Really Matters." *International Journal of Training and Development* 5, pp. 103–20.

Hofstede, G. et al. 2010. *Cultures and Organisations.* New York 2010.

Honey, P., and A. Mumford. 1986. *The Manual of Learning Styles.* Peter Honey Associates, Maidenhead 1986.

Kaltenecker, S. 2017. *Selbstorganisierte Unternehmen.* Heidelberg.

Kaltenecker, S. 2018. *Selbstorganisierte Teams führen.* Heidelberg.

Keysers, C. 2011. "The Empathic Brain." *How the Discovery of Mirror Neurons Changes Our Understanding of Human Nature.* Lexington.

Koch, A. 2017. "Change mich am Arsch." *Wie Unternehmen ihre Mitarbeiter und sich selbst kaputt verändern.* Berlin 2017.

Kolb, D. *Experiential Learning: Experience as the Source of Learning and Development.* New Jersey.

Kübler-Ross, E. 2003. *On Death and Dying.* New York.

Malik, F. 2015. *Managing Performing Living.* Campus.

McLeod, S.A. 2017. "Kolb—Learning Styles." Available online at: www.simplypsychology.org/learning-kolb.html (accessed on January 3, 2019).

Mehrabian, A., and S. Ferris. 1967. "Inference of Attitude from Nonverbal Communication in Two Channels." *The Journal of Counselling Psychology* 31, pp. 248–52.

Meyer, E. 2015. *The Culture Map*. New York.

Mosadeghrad, A.M., and M. Ansarian. 2014. "Why do Organisational Change Programmes Fail?" *International Journal of Strategic Change Management* 5, no. 3, pp. 189–218.

Parianen, F. 2017. *Woher soll ich wissen, was ich denke, bevor ich höre, was ich sage?* Reinbek.

Pink, D. 2009. *Drive*. Riverhead.

Scharmer, C.O. 2018. *The Essentials of Theory U: Core Principles and Applications*. Oaklan.

Schulz von Thun, F. Miteinander reden: Störungen und Klärungen. Bd. 1. Reinbek 2010.

Siefer, W. 2009. *Das Talent in mir. Warum Talent erlernbar ist*. Frankfurt.

Sprenger, R.K. 2010. Mythos Motivation—Wege aus einer Sackgasse. Frankfurt, New York.

Robinson D, S. Perryman, and S. Hayday. 2004. "The Drivers of Employee Engagement," Report 408, Institute for Employment Studies.

Chade-Meng, T. 2014. *Search Inside Yourself*. New York.

Tuckman, B. 1965. "Developmental Sequence in Small Groups." *Psychological Bulletin* 63, pp. 384–99.

Velada, R., A. Caetano, J.W. Michel, B.D. Lyons, M.J. Kavanagh. 2007. "The Effects of Training Design, Individual Characteristics and Work Environment on Transfer of Training." *International Journal of Training and Development* 11, pp. 282–294.

Vermeer, A. 2017. *Selbstorganisierte Teams in der Praxis*. Den Haag 2017.

Wentland, D. 2003. "The Strategic Training of Employees Model: Balancing Organizational Constraints and Training Content." *Advanced Management Journal* 68, pp. 56–63.

Whitmore, J. 2009. *Coaching for Performance: GROWing Human Potential and Purpose—The Principles and Practice of Coaching and Leadership*. London, Boston.

Zenger, J.H., and K. Stinnett. 2010. *The Extraordinary Coach: How the Best Leaders Help Others Grow*. New York.

About the Author

Michael Hagemann has been responsible for change management for several years at the leading global logistics provider, Deutsche Post DHL Group.

After fulfilling various responsibilities in the church as a priest, academic director for international adult education as well as project and change manager for major events, the diploma theologian took a sabbatical and completed a radical, personal re-orientation and evolved himself into a change and transformation manager for positions in consulting, teacher training, and engagement in educational organizations as well as NGOs.

He completed his MBA successfully at the University of Mannheim and ESSEC Paris; his extensive expertise is complemented by numerous training courses and certifications, including as an Advisor (analog Six-Sigma Green Belt), Trainer, Coach, systemic change consultant, DISC Trainer, Mindfulness Practitioner, and NLP Master.

As a sought-after Keynote Speaker, he established and amplified the topic of change management at Deutsche Post DHL Group, took up responsibility for change management in major international programs and for education and continuous further training of a global change practitioner community.

He supports cultural transformation programs and ensures the success of restructuring, implementation, or other numerous change projects as a consultant, trainer, and coach, supported by a wide international team of change practitioners.

E-mail: hagemannmichael@web.de

Index

OTHER TITLES IN THE HUMAN RESOURCE MANAGEMENT AND ORGANIZATIONAL BEHAVIOR COLLECTION

- *Our Glassrooms* by Dhruva Trivedy
- *Creating the Accountability Culture* by Yvonnne Thompson
- *Conflict and Leadership* by Christian Muntean
- *Power Quotes* by Danai Krokou
- *Negotiating with Winning Words* by Michael Schatzki
- *21st Century Skills for Non-Profit Managers* by Don Macdonald and Charles Oham

Announcing the Business Expert Press Digital Library

Concise e-books business students need for classroom and research

This book can also be purchased in an e-book collection by your library as

- a one-time purchase,
- that is owned forever,
- allows for simultaneous readers,
- has no restrictions on printing, and
- can be downloaded as PDFs from within the library community.

Our digital library collections are a great solution to beat the rising cost of textbooks. E-books can be loaded into their course management systems or onto students' e-book readers.
The **Business Expert Press** digital libraries are very affordable, with no obligation to buy in future years. For more information, please visit **www.businessexpertpress.com/librarians**. To set up a trial in the United States, please email **sales@businessexpertpress.com.**

www.ingramcontent.com/pod-product-compliance
Lightning Source LLC
Chambersburg PA
CBHW061322220326
41599CB00026B/4989